The Complete User's Guide To the Amazing Amazon Kindle

By Stephen Windwalker

The bestselling unauthorized guide that will help you get the most out of the revolutionary new e-reader from Amazon

Harvard Perspectives Press

About the Author

Stephen Windwalker, a pen name, is an American author of fiction and nonfiction books, articles, and stories who lives in Arlington, Massachusetts. His previous books include the novel ***Say My Name***, a collection of short fiction entitled ***A Day at the Ballpark and Other Stories***, and the online booksellers' bible ***Selling Used Books Online***.

Windwalker founded the indie publishing company Harvard Perspectives Press in 1999 and named it after two of his favorite institutions from his undergraduate days, the Harvard House of Pizza and the Harvard Wine Company. The press has also published works by M. Robert Gardner and the Parents' Committee for Public Awareness, and he is currently editing ***Before I Knew Any Better***, the debut novel of Alicia Wentworth, which is schedule for publication early in 2009.

Before he adopted his pen name Windwalker served as Fiction Editor of the Harvard Advocate literary magazine, founder of the Dorchester Reading Authority bookstore, and business manager of Inc. Magazine's ancillary book and software publishing division before and during the magazine's purchase by Bertelsmann A.G.

THE BOOK THAT IS HELPING THOUSANDS OF KINDLE OWNERS TO GET THE MOST OUT OF THIS REVOLUTIONARY E-READER THAT IS REALLY *SO MUCH MORE ...*

...by Stephen Windwalker, the man who has learned from his experiences as an author, bookseller, journalist and publishing executive to write the bible on the online bookselling business, and here turns his inquisitive, polymath attention and clear yet elegant writing style to the device that is changing the face and the future of reading.

WHAT OTHERS ARE SAYING ABOUT EARLIER BOOKS BY STEPHEN WINDWALKER....

Stephen Windwalker has done it again.

--Manuel Burgos, author of Graphics on the Kindle

Regarding Windwalker's previous title, *Selling Used Books Online:*

"Incredible business resource.... An experienced authority candidly describes the pitfalls and the realities of ... book dealing with no punches withheld."

--Bob Spear, Heartland Reviews

The Complete User's Guide to the Amazing Amazon Kindle
By Stephen Windwalker

First Edition Paper Original – September 2008.
Harvard Perspectives Press
hppress@gmail.com
Arlington, Massachusetts
hppress.blogspot.com

Unattributed quotations are by Stephen Windwalker.

TABLE OF CONTENTS

Appendices

I. How to Use this Book

Welcome to the world of the amazing Amazon Kindle.

If you've just purchased and received your Kindle, you are in for a treat -- a whole new world of reading, and an astonishing array of other features that you may not have expected.

The purpose of this book is to help you get the most out of your Kindle. With that in mind, let me introduce myself. While most books that are aimed at helping people use gadgets have been written by tech-savvy gadget heads who could probably write their entire books in some sort of mysterious code, this one is different. Like the subject of the amusing P.O.E.M. commercial parodies on Garrison Keillor's weekly radio program, I am an English major. I am also a lifelong reader with decades of experience in the fields of publishing, editing, bookselling, and relatively literate journalism. I've written several books and articles including some very successful material on Amazon and how it conducts its business, but my passion as an author has always been fiction and narrative nonfiction. Most of the people who will buy a Kindle from here on out are likely to be serious readers first and foremost, and thus, kindred spirits. I hope that the way I have approached this book will be a good fit for you. I'm writing for human beings, not gadget heads.

You may want to pace yourself and balance the process of getting to know your Kindle as you work your way through the book. Naturally, you may notice certain limitations that result from the fact that you are reading a paperback copy of a book that was originally written for the electronic medium that is the Kindle. Although I have removed the little "links" at the end of each chapter and section that say "Go Back to Table of Contents" because I can't afford the liability insurance costs I might have to pay if you injure your thumb trying to click on the printed page, I have otherwise left the font style as-is where links exist in the electronic version. If you would like to have access to the links that are featured in the electronic versions of this text, you'll find a complete list at the book blog for this book at **http://kindleusers.blogspot.com**.

I guess I should apologize here for two things. First, production and shipping costs being what they are, I cannot offer the paperback to you free. And second, I hope you won't think it crass hucksterism on my part to suggest that anyone who possesses the Kindle edition might also wish to purchase a paperback copy. I had never thought of such a thing until I heard a podcast of Jeff Bezos and Chris Anderson at the BEA in which Jeff remarked about some significant subset of Kindle owners who buy ***both*** Kindle editions and hardcopy editions of the same titles. I'm still a little perplexed by this, although I certainly understand how it would be helpful with certain types of texts such as, for instance, a reference or how-to book like this one.

Which brings me to another way to use this book, and in this case specifically the paperback edition. It was my original intention to produce a paperback edition, for one simple reason:

If you are considering buying a Kindle (or anything else for that matter) for the first time for $359, it makes all the sense in the world to conduct due diligence beforehand. While my primary intent here is to provide a guide for Kindle users, I sincerely hope that the paperback version will also be a worthwhile way for prospective buyers to conduct that due-diligence research and find out exactly what they can expect of the Kindle should they buy one.

If you are among this number, you may want, as you consider the possible purchase of a Kindle, to supplement the information-gathering process that you are beginning, with this book, by getting a look at a Kindle and its features, in the real world. This may seem like a challenge, since Amazon doesn't have any physical stores and Amazon is the only authorized seller of the Kindle, but the Kindle's marketing team has rolled out a potential fix for this problem. The Kindle Store now features a "See a Kindle in Your City" section with links to Kindles in a long and growing list of cities and towns to help you connect with Kindle owners and see the device in person.

* * *

As you are probably aware, Amazon also provides several useful documents along with the Kindle, including a brief "About Your Kindle" start-up guide that comes in the box with the Kindle, a basic Kindle User's Guide that you will find on your Kindle when you turn it on (but you can also download it to your computer and even print it out as a .pdf file from Amazon's website), and a License

Agreement with terms and conditions that is provided as an in-the-box hard copy and can also be viewed on Amazon's website.

Please be sure to read these documents from Amazon and make appropriate use of Amazon's Kindle Support program. This book is intended to supplement the materials that you will receive from Amazon, not to replace them. I understand that you are eager to begin reading other content on your Kindle, but the little bit of time that you will spend learning to navigate the device is bound to pay off during the many years of enjoyment you will get from your new Kindle.

* * *

I am not going to insult you by asking you to wade through multiple pages that tell you what to expect in Chapter 1, what to expect in Chapter 2, and so forth. However, given the myriad ways in which Kindle owners are using their Kindles, there is a certain organizational challenge in trying to bring order to a project such as this book. For instance, Kindle owners who are otherwise lucky enough to live permanently in rural or exurban areas not yet graced with wireless Whispernet service might not expect to find information on how to get their Kindle content onto their Kindles in a chapter about ***traveling*** with the Kindle, since they do not have to travel to face this challenge. However, that's where I have put it. So I simply urge you to begin by familiarizing yourself with this book's Table of Contents (at the beginning) and the Frequently Asked Questions (at the end) sections of the book, each of which is extensively linked to specific areas of content within the book. And go from there.

If you conclude that I have left out something important and potentially useful, I hope that you will consider dropping me an email at indieKindle@gmail.com. Let me know your thoughts, and I will make every effort to be responsive, both specifically to you and more publicly in a future edition of this book.

* * *

Let me say a few words about using the links that are embedded copiously throughout this text, since they are included as an intended convenience, and not as a gratuitous annoyance.

First, with respect to internal links that help you navigate to another section in the text, I will note simply that you can always get back immediately to the location at which you were reading before you clicked on the internal link by pressing the "back" button on the right side of your Kindle, just below the "Next Page" bar.

Second, with respect to the external links that would take you from the text of this book to other websites, these can slow you down considerably and fill up your Kindle's web cache, so I recommend using them judiciously. Sometimes you will find that you need to use the menu and scroll-wheel to click on "reload" to see this web content, and other times, as with many Amazon pages, the web browser will simply take you to Amazon and show you a message that it "couldn't find" the page in question. (If this happens, you may want to wait a few more seconds before you give up on the page). This does not mean I am using a dead link, but is instead a limitation of the Kindle's browser. You may find it much more convenient to send me a request for a Word attachment so that you can access these links directly from your computer. I will be happy to oblige, but -- for reasons I hope you can understand -- only if you follow the exact instructions that you may find by clicking here.

II. What is a Kindle?

I remember thinking it was cool a few years back when one or two online booksellers began featuring same-day book delivery on the island of Manhattan. I read a lot, and it always appeals to me to begin reading something new as soon as I hear about it. It almost made me want to move to New York.

Anyway, for anyone who thought same-day delivery was cool, consider the Kindle. We are talking ***same-minute delivery*** here, almost anywhere in the United States, for the world's largest electronic book catalog -- over 160,000 titles, and growing now by more than 25,000 titles a month!

Although the content that you will purchase from the Kindle store is protected with Digital Rights Management (DRM), Kindle owners can clip, annotate, snip, highlight and bookmark any of that content so that it is automatically saved to their "My Clippings" folders, from which they can transfer it to their computers instantaneously via USB cable and edit, print, save, cut and paste, email, or otherwise work with it as they would any other text file on their computers' hard drives.

And it's so green, the Gore family must have one in every room. No paper, no trees, no energy-sucking book warehouses, no freight or fuel, and very, very little electricity. You can even take the Kindle outside and read while you are enjoying that same Mother Nature that you are helping to protect, since the Kindle's e-Ink display is not backlit and is eminently readable even in outdoor light.

The Kindle is an electronic reading device manufactured by Amazon and launched in November 2007 at an initial retail price of $399, reduced a few months later to $359. It comes with a one-year warranty and is a decidedly unimposing, not very elegant gadget in an off-white plastic case with a QWERTY keyboard so tiny that you may not notice that it's there until you accidentally hit a key that causes the Kindle to navigate somewhere. The device is configured to work with a proprietary format (.azw) created by Amazon in order to allow Amazon to control Digital Rights Management (DRM) to protect itself and the authors and publishers who make content available through the Kindle store. However, Amazon will also convert other files including personal documents that you send to your Kindle email address in text, Word, html, .prd, .mobi, or image format. I've even had consistent success sending .pdf documents to my Kindle email address for conversion by Amazon and reading them on the device, despite the fact that Amazon refers to its .pdf conversion feature as "experimental."

Although the Kindle has generated a lot of buzz in the first year since it is launch, there are many ways in which it has experienced a very quiet beginning. Amazon hasn't advertised it anywhere beyond its own web site and Google ads sprinkled around the web.

There are several hundred thousand Kindles up and running in the wild, but just try and find one. It is a lot like the Prius in, say, 2002. You've heard it is the next new thing, but you never see one. (Update: As I was proofreading this chapter today, I got a call from my friend Paul, who works as a bartender at an upscale Boston seafood restaurant and told me that he now sees a Kindle at the bar on the average of one per day, each in the hands of a different patron. I don't know what it is about Legal Seafood, but I need to make sure that Paul is getting the job done for me, as a buzz agent, with all these Kindlers!)

Still, Amazon seems to know it has a keeper. Look at what they named it. The word "kindle" conjures up images of a prairie fire, revolutionary change, even ***Fahrenheit 451***.

What's Inside the Kindle?

But let's keep it simple and start by running down the basic elements of the hardware. The first thing to know is that the Kindle is a computer. Because it is built on the Linux platform, its creators have been able to provide a very specific and targeted range of features in a stripped down, technologically economical package whose native 64MB of memory and 256MB of storage are reminiscent of the computers of the 1980s. Here is what's inside the Kindle:

* CPU: The Kindle's "brain" is an Intel PXA255 processor, originally designed for smart phones.

* e-Ink Display: There's a reason why the Kindle doesn't do color. Its e-Ink display involves millions of microcapsules that act as pixels that provide a sharp but easy-on-the-eyes black, white and gray

display on the Kindle's 600x800-pixel screen. These microcapsules are driven by a layer of transparent electrodes that consume far less power than LCD displays.

* Operating System: Your Kindle's operating system is a modified Linux 2.6.10 kernel. Amazon has complied with Linux licensing by making its modified source code freely available. Among the modifications is support for XIP (execute in place), a feature that promotes more efficient, faster use of the system's memory.

* Memory: Your Kindle is equipped with 256 MB internal flash memory. About two-thirds of this memory is available for storing your documents, music, bookmarks, photographs, notes, and anything else you choose to store on your Kindle. The easiest way to see how this memory is being utilized is to check the "Kindle drive" while it is connected via USB to your desktop or notebook computer. You can greatly multiply the storage that your Kindle can access by adding an SD memory card - here's a link: **http://www.amazon.com/exec/obidos/ASIN/B000EOMXM0/ebest**

* Battery: You can get the most out of your Kindle's replaceable lithium-polymer battery -- as much as one week on a single charge -- if you keep the wireless feature switched off whenever you aren't using it. But it is not a bad idea to order a replacement battery just so you have one handy in the event of a malfunction - here's a link: **http://www.amazon.com/exec/obidos/ASIN/B000I6P1UA/ebest**

* Connectivity: The service that Amazon calls Whispernet is actually a 3G EVDO wireless broadband service through an AnyDate modem that enables the Kindle to connect to Sprint's United States wireless data network. This service is available in most densely populated areas, but not everywhere. For more information about this service read The Amazon Kindle Basic Web Wireless Service. The Kindle also comes with a USB cable for easy connection to your desktop or laptop computer.

Although the Kindle has been marketed initially as an "e-book reader," its array of features actually sets the bar considerably higher than any of its predecessor e-book devices. Electronic reading devices have been around for decades, but until the launch of the Kindle they failed to gain any serious traction.

These ancillary Kindle features include audio, graphic, and even game-playing capacities, but foremost among them is the Kindle's free broadband wireless connectivity (via the Sprint 3G EV-DO service), which has significant benefits for the device's functionality both with e-books and with other content. Such a data connection ordinarily costs over $50 per month, but Amazon pays the entire bill (whatever it is), handles any problems with Sprint, and uses the connection to run a "Whispernet" service that allows Kindle owners to download content -- books, newspapers, magazines, and blogs -- within seconds of purchasing it from the Kindle store.

In addition to this wireless connectivity and nearly instantaneous content delivery, of course, the Kindle's viability as a reading device owes a great deal to the fact that it is manufactured and sold by Amazon. Over the 13 years prior to its launch of the Kindle, Amazon built enormous brand power among book buyers and book publishers, with over 50 million visitors each month (the lion's share of whom still think of Amazon as a bookseller despite its relentlessly expanding product mix), a catalog of over 4 million book titles, and business relationships with thousands of publishers and authors.

What does this marketplace power mean for the future of the Kindle?

The tens of millions of readers who visit the main Amazon store to find books and other items each month are invariably shown enticing text and graphics about the Kindle. The installed base of Kindle users is approaching 1% of the installed base of all Amazon customers as I write these words, and will likely reach 3% in 2009 and 6% in 2010. To speculate that it will not keep growing steadily through the next decade would be to assume that the technology, marketing, and marketplace muscle that have brought the Kindle this far will somehow slow to near-stasis. This is not likely.

The thousands of publishers who do business with Amazon, from Random House down to self-published authors with a single title, are regularly invited to make their content available in Kindle editions. Amazon's goal for the Kindle catalog is that it will ultimately give readers access to "every book ever printed." Although large and small publishers have some history of complaint about Amazon tactics and revenue splits, they also have a clear history of nearly universal participation in Amazon's bookselling opportunities. No serious business enterprise can afford to leave the amounts of money represented by Amazon's growing market share on the table.

And for Kindle owners who search for titles that are not yet available in Kindle editions, Amazon now provides a handy little above-the-fold widget, complete with a miniature picture of a

Kindle, allowing a single click to "Please tell the publisher: I'd like to read this book on Kindle."

While it may take some imagination and a stunning upward curve to plot progress from the Kindle store's initial, seemingly rather plodding title growth (88,000 titles at launch up to 160,000 titles in August 2008) to the aforementioned "every book ever printed" standard, Amazon also has access to the cash and stock that it might need to make any deals necessary to buy into other ventures such as the Open Content Alliance and Google Books to digitalize "every book ever printed." Even if such efforts currently seem at odds with Amazon's Digital Rights Management and revenue structures for the Kindle, these boundaries, alliances, and oppositions have a way of changing as technologies change.

No other e-book manufacturer, handheld device manufacturer, or content digitizer has anything like these powers that Amazon possesses. Amazon's marketplace muscle more than offsets the Kindle's first-generation flaws, and early indications are that the Kindle's first-year success is causing significant loss of market share and traction for relatively worthy competitors such as Sony's e-Reader.

Despite Steve Jobs' bizarre claim that the Kindle is a non-starter because people don't read books any more, the Kindle's most powerful direct hardware competition is bound to come from the iPhone, the iPod Touch, other Apple products, and other smartphones such as the Blackberry. The elegance of these devices, their domination of the marketplace in their categories, and the increasingly open access to their code and platforms goes a long way toward offsetting their manufacturers' lack of positioning in the book publishing and bookselling marketplaces and the fact their display screens are not well-suited to long-form reading. Over 100 million people own these devices, and small yet growing and significant numbers of people are likely to use them for reading if content is sufficiently available. Although people who own these devices are far less likely to spend a significant amount of time buying and reading books on them (given the appeal of their other features) than people who own Kindles, it is certainly meaningful, nonetheless, that Fictionwise was quoted in Publisher's Weekly in mid-August that its eReader software had been installed on 130,000 iPhone/iPod Touch devices and 35,000 of that group had purchased e-books from Fictionwise.com, less than two months after eReader was made available in Apple's iPhone Apps store.

Techie blogs and other similar venues are likely to be polluted for months or even years to come with the claims and counter claims of Macphiles, Kindlers, stock short-sellers and others about the ugliness or elegance of the Kindle, exactly when, how, and where Apple will announce the launch of the device that will be the ultimate Kindle Killer, when Apple or Amazon will achieve world domination, and why it is clear that Amazon has actually sold and shipped only 674 Kindles in the device's first year following launch.

Enough already. All these people (actually I think there are only 674 of them, but like the people who write 1-star reviews of this book, they have 674 screen names each) have an agenda. Not that there is anything wrong with that.

But the fact is that Amazon and Apple do tens of millions of dollars of business with each other, they will do even more business with each other in the future, and the vast majority of people who own Kindles also own one or more Apple products as well. Although it is unlikely that we will ever see anything that we might confuse as a "marriage" of Amazon and Apple, the future is very likely to feature increasing interaction between Kindle content and Apple devices. While it may make great business sense for Apple to limit its devices' new-purchase electronic entertainment access to music and movies that they buy in the iTunes store, it would make no sense at all for Apple and Amazon to refuse to co-operate in finding ways to make Kindle editions of digitalized text accessible to iPhone and iPod owners through agreements that would be highly profitable to both companies.

Given that Amazon already provides a significant 10% Amazon Associates "affiliate fee" to business partners who provide the links that result in any and all purchases from the Kindle Store, working out the numbers for an Apple-Kindle Store partnership may be as simple as engineering a kind of reverse affiliate fee, for Apple, for all Kindle content that is sold to any Apple device. But of course it is never that simple.

It's easy, in this kind of discussion, to fall into a "wag the dog" kind of confusion about whether the hardware, the software, or the content is the dominant and game-changing element. It all depends. Since the fact that we are even having these conversations results from the launch of the Kindle as a hardware device in November 2007, it is natural enough to focus on hardware. Indeed, by launching the hardware and finally giving real traction to the development of interest in an electronic reader after decades in which e-books were an unfulfilled technological promise, Amazon has placed itself squarely at the head of the table when it comes to creating the standards for future e-reader feature sets, reading experience, content delivery, connectivity, and even product look and feel.

That is a huge triumph in market positioning and branding, but it does not in and of itself make clear that revenue from the sale of Kindle hardware is now, or ever will be, more important to Amazon than revenue from the "Kindle edition" content sold and delivered through the "Kindle store." Naturally, given a choice, Amazon will want both. But my sense is that, in addition to all the ways in which it is fun and energizing for Jeff Bezos and thousands of Amazon employees to have shared in launching this cool device, the real narrative behind the Kindle's importance for Amazon involves a different kind of market positioning, back story, and vision of the future.

When Amazon announced the Kindle, Bezos said the product had been three years in development, placing its gestation roughly in late 2004. By late 2004, what had Amazon achieved?

it had been in business for a decade and had begun turning quarterly and annual profits after dozens of quarters in which it had frightened market analysts with its insouciant attitude about short-term profitability;

it had created the greatest bookselling success story in the history of the book and had positioned itself as the largest single retailer on the Internet;

it had made its founder one of the richest young self-made men in the world, distinguished him as a certified business visionary, and placed him on Time Magazine's cover as its Man of the Year (in 1999, while he was still in his 30s); and

it had, more than any other single business, already given rise to a concept that will be one of the defining business and cultural principles of the 21st century -- "the long tail" as codified and explained in Chris Anderson's 2006 bestseller of the same title -- which can be crudely summed up as the idea that a global Internet company could find it more profitable to offer millions of distinct products (and providing its customers with convenient ways to find those products and share them with others) than it would to provide unlimited quantities of, say, its top 300 titles (think, the book department at Wal-Mart).

Not bad at all for a start-up Web 1.0 company. However, while it might be melodramatic to assert that there were dark clouds on the Amazon horizon in 2004, it would certainly be fair to say that the company's continuing market dominance was far from guaranteed. Simply continuing to do what it had done so well throughout its first decade in business would lead to atrophy, declining sales, losses, and ultimate extinction.

In addition to the much-discussed and possibly over-hyped threat of a declining population of book readers, the greater threat existed in ideas that were quickly gaining traction and interest with projects such as Google Books and, a few months later, the Open Content Alliance. If these players were about the business of digitalizing every book ever printed, to the extent that copyright law would allow, what would it mean for Amazon? It might mean different things, and certainly one could argue that Amazon's sales of traditional, print-on-paper, dead-tree books might be enhanced for a while at least if readers could search for and read portions of their content online. However, it was at least equally probable that Amazon would sell fewer such books over time as a result of all this digitalizing, or digitizing, or whatever is the correct verb in its gerundive form.

Instead of watchful waiting, Amazon made a fascinating decision: overcoming any hesitation that might have been justified by the prior failure of e-readers to take off in any meaningful way, Amazon made a major corporate commitment to the development of a revolutionary new digital reading device that would invite readers to enjoy digital content -- books, mainly -- in a reading mode as nearly similar as possible or imaginable to the actual experience of reading a book.

By taking control of the hardware interface, enhancing it with appealing features, and beating potential competitors to the punch with content that would quickly include a high percentage of bestsellers, cheaply available public-domain classics, a growing and representative sampling of mid-list titles, and some of the most popular newspapers, magazines, and blogs, Amazon changed whatever games that had been initiated by Google Book Search, the Open Content Alliance, and predecessor e-book manufacturers.

For the near term, certainly, the Kindle will remain an important product as Amazon's first foray into the realm of hardware manufacturing. But five years or ten years out, the question is open whether the hardware will be anywhere near as important to Amazon as the content. If Amazon can use the Kindle as a Trojan horse to set the standards and feature sets that human readers expect to find in an electronic reading device, and fortify its already dominant position as the leading content provider for such devices, much of the Kindle's work will be done. At that point if not sooner, there is no reason to think that Amazon would not open its big tent to let a thousand e-reader flowers bloom. After all, it would only require a mid single-digits percentage of iPod, iPhone, and Blackberry owners buying content from the Kindle Store to surpass the overall content purchasing level of all Kindle owners, even several years out. If any of these brands offers hardware with a larger display and more hospitable form factor for long-form reading, they could indeed, strictly from a hardware perspective, "outKindle the Kindle." Yet, even if they do surpass the Kindle at some point, Amazon's market position is probably sufficient to ensure both that sales of the Kindle hardware will continue to grow and, more important, that the Kindle Store's content offerings, once they are made available, will be the most popular content offerings on all such devices.

Nothing, including my outlandishly hopeful and optimistic suggestion of a coming alliance between the Kindle and Apple's i-devices, is at all clear about how things will transpire in the world of digital reading. But Amazon has a leg up, and it should be able to combine what it has achieved with the Kindle and with its customer loyalty and its previous 14 years of success in the bookselling marketplace to ensure that it will continue to be a major provider of book content on and off the printed page for the next few decades.

Okay, you've noticed. I began this chapter intending to describe what the Kindle is, and I ended up in a rapture of imagination about what it can become. But it's not me.

It's the Kindle.

The Kindle isn't exactly cool. It certainly isn't pretty. But a decade from now the people who make such pronouncements will look back on the 2007 Kindle and declare that it was a major turning point in the cultural and technological changes of the early 21st century.

The kindling point.

Why Did Amazon Launch the Kindle, and Which is More Important, the Chicken or the Egg?

There is another, perhaps more direct way to approach all this: by looking at Jeff Bezos' own words.

I've finally gotten around to transcribing this remarkable but brief exchange between Chris Anderson and Jeff Bezos at the 2008 Book Expo America. You can check my transcription and listen to the entire podcast here, but in my view it is this exchange which states most clearly that the primary importance of the Kindle for Amazon lies in four things: it jumpstarts significant electronic book sales; it positions the books in the Kindle store as the primary source of e-reader content; it sets the bar higher than it had previously been set for form factor, feature set, and delivery mode for electronic books; and it gives Amazon a seat at the head of the table in shaping this area of book commerce going forward.

Q. "In Asia, [there are] cell phone serials, cell phone comics, cell phone mangas, etc. I guess, first question, what have you learned from the mobile reading experience in Asia? Secondly, does that in itself put the Kindle in competition with the cell phone down the line as cell phones have better screens, etc."

--Chris Anderson, author of The Long Tail

A. "Maybe the hardware device, yes, but not necessarily the Kindle books. The Kindle books, maybe they should be available on every device. We created Kindle because we've been selling e-Books for 10 years, but we needed an electron microscope to find the sales. And so, three years ago we said, Look, what we need to do is create a perfect, integrated, streamlined customer experience all the way through, so we'll build the device, we'll build the back-end servers, we'll digitize the content ourselves if we need to. Whatever it takes, we're going to build a great customer experience, to get that thing started. If we can get other devices to also be able to buy Kindle books, through other devices, that's great."

--Jeff Bezos, CEO of Amazon

III. Kindle Basics

A. Handling Your Kindle

Once you've opened your Kindle's elegant packaging and turned on the two switches on the back cover, you are ready to begin enjoying it. Please be sure to read the Kindle User's Guide that has been preloaded to the Kindle -- it is a quick read, and as I've said earlier, ***this*** book is intended to supplement Amazon's documentation rather than to duplicate it.

I'm not going to try to tell you how to hold the Kindle -- each Kindle owner should find his or her own most comfortable reading postures, which are likely to vary anyway depending on whether you are reading in bed, on a flight, at the breakfast table, on a cardio machine at the gym, or -- well, let's hope you catch my drift before I start sounding like Dr. Seuss (you cannot hold it in a box, you must not keep it with your socks!).

In addition to the all-important display screen, the key elements to locate on your Kindle are the "previous page" and "next page" buttons, the "back" button, the "Select" scroll-wheel that works like the clickable track-wheel on a mouse, the eerie silvery cursor bar, and the thumb-confounding keyboard.

On the back, of all places, you will find on/off switches for the Kindle and its wireless feature as well as the Kindle's on-board speaker and a removable cover that protects the reset pinhole, the battery, and the SD card slot.

At the Kindle's bottom edge are a standard audio output jack, volume controls, the USB port, the power adapter recharge jack, and a recharge indicator light (it will show amber when charging and will go out when fully charged or when it is not connected). Check battery status as well as Whispernet signal strength with the "bars" indicators that should always be present at the bottom of the Kindle's display screen except when it is asleep or booting up.

There is probably no single complaint that gets more discussion among new Kindle 1.0 users than the difficulty of handling the Kindle without constantly making undesired contact with the unnecessarily large and prominent "PREV PAGE" and "NEXT

PAGE" bars on either side of the device and, thus, losing one's place in whatever one is reading. I won't try to write anything that takes the place of all this discussion, but I will add two specific thoughts to the colloquy.

1. As with almost anything else, one adapts to this problem over time. It is certainly a design flaw that needs attention in Kindle 2.0, but must admit that I have found that I have gotten better at handling the Kindle in ways that avoid this problem.

2. I've noticed that I do best at handling my Kindle when it is in its original black Kindle cover, with the black elasticized "holder" strap tucked diagonally over the lower right-hand corner of the device, just below the "Back" button. If I arrange the strap at a certain angle, it doesn't even hide the "aA" and "Enter/Return" keys.

B. Choosing Among Six Font Sizes

The Kindle can vastly improve the reading experience for those of us who are challenged by small font sizes. Tap the "aA" key at the far right of the keyboard's bottom row and you'll be shown an array of six font sizes. Just use the scroll wheel to select the font size that is right for you. This feature generally works in Kindle documents and on the web, but won't work with the Home screen, screen shots, graphic representations of text, Kindle menus or settings pages, or pages in the Kindle store.

Although this can vary somewhat based on formatting embedded by a publisher, the six font sizes correspond to type fonts that are 7, 9, 11, 14, 17 and 20-point. Most print-on-paper books use fonts that are in the 10-to-12-point range.

Tip: Using a larger font size while you are working on the web or checking your email can also be helpful by making it easier to keep hyperlinks separate.

Tip: Using a smaller font size when you are working with clippings or annotations can allow you to capture more text.

C. Kindle Keyboard and Menu Shortcuts

It will take you about five minutes to learn the basics of Kindle navigation, but if you are at all like me you will also find it helpful to keep returning to this chapter to refresh your memory about how to use a keyboard shortcut to get somewhere you only visit occasionally.

The trick to getting the hang of these shortcuts and commands is to familiarize yourself with the bottom row of the Kindle keyboard and the special powers of the keys that you will find there, and then to learn how to use keyboard combinations (built primarily on the ALT, SHIFT, and @ keys) to get places fast and conduct more powerful operations.

For many Kindle owners, the keyboard is something to be avoided. They are here to read, after all. But in between books, the keyboard can be the gateway to dozens of other Kindle features that add to the power and utility of this remarkable gadget. Just as important, the keyboard can help you navigate more effectively while you are reading a Kindle book or other content, and it can come in handy when you want to make some notes on what you are reading so you can check back later, save them, or share them with a colleague or another reader.

In the section below, whenever you find a command that begins with ALT-SHIFT, you must hold the ALT and SHIFT keys down simultaneously (rather than consecutively) and press the next key at the same time. Fortunately, the ALT and SHIFT keys are abutters, so that you will should be able to carry out this operation without a third thumb.

General

ALT-aA: SLEEP Mode

ALT-SHIFT-R: Reboot (Keyboard Reset)

SYM: Show additional symbols for keyboard typing

ALT-T: Get time (text from Kindle document reader; numerical elsewhere)

ALT-Z: Rescan files and subdirectories in directory named "pictures" for recognition by Kindle as "book" files

ALT-SHIFT-M: Start "Minesweeper" Game (from Home screen)

From the Kindle Reader

aA: Adjust Font Size

J (from the "Adjust Font Size" screen): Show/Hide toggle for text justification options

ALT-B: Toggle bookmarking of the current page

ALT-T: See current time in text format at bottom of screen

ALT-0: Sets screen-view slideshow in "On" position (but does not begin it)

ALT-1: Begin slideshow (if on)

ALT-2: End slideshow

ALT-NEXT PAGE or ALT-PREV PAGE: Move quickly forward or backward in a document; you will move either to the next bookmarked location or in a 1/20th chunk

ALT-SHIFT-G: Save Screenshot to SD Memory Card as .GIF file

GPS Commands From the Browser

ALT-1: Show current location using Google Maps

ALT-2: Find gas stations nearby using Google Maps

ALT-3: Find restaurants nearby using Google Maps

ALT-4 and ALT-5: Find "Enter your custom keyword here" nearby using Google Maps

From the Keyboard

<- (BACKSPACE): Clear last character and set cursor at that location

ALT-<- (BACKSPACE): Clear all characters in input field

ALT-H: Move cursor left one space without clearing character

ALT-J: Move cursor right one space without clearing character

SYM: Show additional symbols for keyboard typing, including:

ALT-6: ?

ALT-7: ,

ALT-8::

ALT-9: "

ALT-0: '

From the Audio Player

ALT-F: Skip to Next Track

ALT-P: Play/Stop Toggle

From the Search Line

Limit your Kindle search to specific universes such as the Kindle Store, Wikipedia, or the web by typing your search term into the search field preceded by the following prefixes and a space:

@web: Web Browser

@wiki: Wikipedia

@store: Kindle Store

@time: Time

@help: List of supported "@" shortcuts

From the Picture Viewer

ALT-SHIFT-0: Set current picture as screen saver (erases native Kindle screen savers)

F: Toggle full-screen mode

To remove custom screen savers from your Kindle, connect the Kindle to your computer via USB, go into the "System" folder and then into the "screen_saver" folder. Delete all files from that folder.

From the Settings Page

411: Run Kindle device diagnostics

511: Run loopback call test

611: Diagnostic data service call

126: Lab 126 Team Member credit roll

D. The Care and Feeding of Your Kindle's Battery

Among the numerous features that make the Kindle a "green" device is the fact that its battery has great staying power and requires precious little electricity for a recharge. You can check battery status as well as your Whispernet signal strength with the "bars" indicators that should always be present at the bottom of the Kindle's display screen except when it is asleep or booting up. (When the Kindle is recharging, the battery strength indicator will be replaced with a little "lightning bolt" graphic.)

Recharging a Kindle's battery via the power adapter is a relatively quick process that usually requires less than two hours. Two recommendations that seem to work for many Kindle owners are (1) recharge your Kindle at the same time each day or evening so that it becomes a regular routine and you always begin the day with a fully charged device; and (2) except when you are traveling, always recharge your Kindle in the same outlet and keep the power adapter there so that you will be less likely to misplace it.

The Kindle comes with an AC cord to recharge its battery directly from a conventional U.S. power outlet. Charge the battery up when you first get your Kindle, and generally it should give you back something close to Amazon's claims of one-day battery life when the wireless switch is "on" and up to one week of battery life when the wireless switch is "off."

Obviously, the most important thing you can do to save your battery life is to keep the wireless switch "off" when you aren't using the wireless. It only takes a few seconds to connect when you switch it back on.

If you plan to travel a lot with your Kindle or generally use it away from home, it may well be a good investment to pay $20 for an alternate battery. Gomadic also sells a convenient "Emergency AA Battery Charge Extender" for the Kindle right on the Amazon site. Another vendor, iGo Everywhere, offers several different Kindle chargers and a kit that includes both a wall (AC) and automotive (DC) charger as well as retractable cable.

E. The Reset Button is Your First Tech Support Option

I would be remiss if I didn't tell you that my first Kindle froze up -- screen and/or keyboard -- a little more often than I would like. My son's Kindle never freezes, and I do not know what causes the problem with mine. But whenever this or anything else of a negative nature has occurred, I have been able to "fix" it and restore my Kindle to normal operation within seconds by using the "reset" button.

There are two problems with this. First, using the reset button clears the web browser's cache, which in turn means, just as one example, that I have to re-type my user ID and password to check my email on Gmail. Second, it isn't easy to connect with, or for that matter even find, the reset button. But it is there.

Where? Just remove the Kindle's back cover and you'll see a tiny pinhole just to the left of the FCC ID number below the Kindle's two bar codes. I make a point of carrying around either a paper clip or a pushpin that can be inserted easily into that pinhole. When you insert it and give a little push, you will notice a little click of resistance and pushback to let you know you have achieved a successful reset. When you replace the back cover and look at the screen, you will see the silvery cursor bar doing its hourglass thing and climbing and filling in the entire slot at the right of the screen as the system resets and reboots, which takes, on my Kindle, about 75 seconds. Avoid using a pen as a reset device; it will create unwanted guck inside your Kindle, and the point will probably be too big anyway.

If you reset your Kindle and it still does not work, your next step should be to make sure the Kindle battery is properly charged. Then, then call the Kindle support number at 1-866-216-1072.

F. Access Wikipedia Quickly and Smoothly

There is more than one way to get to Wikipedia on the Kindle. Since Wikipedia is a website to which you have probably already navigated many times on your computer, it might seem that the best way to get there is to open the Kindle's Experimental Web Browser and use the Wikipedia bookmark that Amazon has placed there. No. That route will take much longer and may well deliver you to a huge, slow-to-load Wikipedia main page on which navigation and the mere entry of a search term will be slower than molasses, so slow that it may freeze your Kindle by overloading its native (RAM) memory.

Instead, from anywhere on your Kindle, just hit the SEARCH key on the bottom row of your keyboard. Make sure that the wireless switch on the back of the Kindle is in the "ON" position, type the "@wiki", followed by a space and the word or term for which you want to check the Wikipedia, and use the scroll wheel to click on "Go" at the right of the Search line. In a few seconds you will see the Wikipedia listing for the term you have entered, if one exists. (When you arrive at a Wikipedia page you may find it is rather cluttered for the Kindle's display. If your visual acuity permits, I recommend using the "aA" button at the bottom right of the keyboard to reduce the font size so that you are able to see a larger portion of the Wikipedia listing on each Kindle display "page".

If you prefer to search beyond Wikipedia and see what you can find in your Kindle content, in your Kindle's dictionary, and on the web, follow the same process without the "@wiki" prefix. (You do not need to turn on your wireless switch if you are interested only in listings that are already on your Kindle or in your Kindle dictionary.) Your Kindle screen will give you a choice of places to find the word or term: among documents already on your Kindle, in the Kindle's recognized dictionary, on Wikipedia, elsewhere on the web, and in the Kindle store. Just click on any of the other alternatives and you will be there.

G. Using "Locations" to Figure Out How Close You Are to the End of a Kindle Edition

One thing that takes some getting used to, as we make the transition from traditional print-on-paper books to the Kindle, is that we can no longer rely on the two most familiar tools that tell us how far we are from the end of a book or any other document. Most of us get some satisfaction from using page numbers or even the thickness of the remaining pages to conduct and constantly recalculate how near we are to the triumph of completion. For decades I have employed a somewhat perverse habit of checking the final page number when I start reading a book, dividing the total into tenths, and requiring of myself that I get at least to the next fractional benchmark before closing the covers on any book-reading session. When my son Danny was anticipating the arrival of his own personal Kindle, he wondered aloud what he would do about the regular homework assignments that called upon him to read 20 pages a day in whatever book he was reading at the time.

Judging from the number of Amazon Kindle discussion forum posts about the Kindle's lack of "page numbers," Danny and I are not alone. The Kindle may not specifically solve Danny's problem, but it does offer two tools that make it relatively easy to monitor one's reading progress within any text:

* the first, which you've already discovered because it is right at the bottom of the Kindle screen on any text that you read, is the little row of dots that is so intuitive and obvious that I shall not bother typing a line of "guide-speak" gobbledygook to explain how they work: they tell you, proportionally, where you are in whatever you are reading.

* the second is much closer to the actual process of using page numbers. As you have noticed, the Kindle uses "location numbers" rather than page numbers to mark place in any document, for the simple reason that providing traditional pagination is inconsistent with the Kindle's feature that allows you to choose from among six different font sizes. No doubt you have noticed the reference to "Locations 1392-1394," or whatever, in the lower left corner of your Kindle screen when you are reading something. But you may not have noticed how easy it is to find out the exact number of locations in a Kindle edition. Just use the Kindle's scroll-wheel to click on "Menu" from within any Kindle title, and choose "Go to Location" from the pop-up menu. The input box that appears on your screen will show the full range of locations available, e.g., "Location 1 to 3858." In other words, figuring out how many "locations" are contained in any document you are reading is about as easy as checking the page number of the final page of a traditional book. And once you know that number, of course, you are well on the way to figuring out how close you are to finishing, or even, in my case, to setting must-read benchmarks within a given book.

The remaining problem, of course, is that neither of these tools will help you figure out how close you are to the end of the chapter you are reading. In a ebook such as this one with an extensively hyperlinked and interactive table of contents, it is easy to navigate within the book to see where chapters begin and end. If, instead, you are reading a novel or other ebooks that lacks a hyperlinked table of contents, you can always spend a little time, once you commit yourself to reading the whole book, to utilizing the Kindle's page-bookmarking feature to set bookmarks at the beginning of each chapter, or anywhere else for that matter.

H. Buying and Sampling Content for Your Kindle From the Amazon Kindle Store

While the Kindle opens up a vast world of free content in the form of public domain books, blogs, website content and documents that you and others can share directly via your kindle.com email addresses, most Kindle owners purchase the lion's share of their Kindle reading content from Amazon's Kindle Store. If you are browsing and shopping on your home, office or mobile computer, just check out the store and you can choose Kindle Books, Kindle Newspapers, Kindle Magazines, Kindle Blogs, Kindle Store and Kindle Accessories easily from the tabs across the top of the screen. You will also find helpful tab links to Kindle Support and Kindle Discussions, as well as a "Manage Your Kindle" link.

You can also browse and purchase Kindle edition content directly with your Kindle. Although many Kindle owners prefer to make many of their Kindle content purchases from their computers so they can use the full-featured Amazon product detail pages to which they have grown accustomed, there will also be plenty of times when you may find it convenient to use your Kindle's menu selection "Shop in the Kindle store" to sample content or make a purchase immediately. When you take this route, you are bound to be amazed by the speed and seamlessness with which Amazon delivers Kindle content to your device within seconds via the Kindle's Whispernet wireless network.

Before shopping for or with your Kindle, you may want to streamline the experience in advance by going into "Your Amazon Account" to make sure that your payment information and 1-click purchase settings are correct and up-to-date. If you allow it, the Kindle will routinely use your 1-click settings to charge your credit or debit card. If you apply a gift certificate or gift card to your account via your computer, any remaining balance on such an account will be charged for your Kindle purchases before your credit or debit card is charged, but the Kindle will not tell you that during the purchase process.

Before you spend your entire nest egg on Kindle content, you should keep two things in mind:

First, try out the Kindle's terrific **sampling** feature. Whether you are browsing titles directly from your Kindle or on your computer, the Kindle edition detail page for just about any title in the Kindle store will show a button on the right that allows you to send a sample chapter or two (usually up to 5% of the full text) directly, and pretty much instantly, to your Kindle. What's not to like about that?

Second, it is well worth checking out a website such as ManyBooks to explore the remarkable selection of **free content** that you will be able to download to your Kindle. This site is wonderfully user-friendly -- just find a title by author, title, or the search field, select "Kindle" from the pull-down list of available formats, click on download, and the title will be on your computer drive within seconds so that you can shoot it on to your Kindle email address (or transfer it via USB) in another 15 seconds or so.

Tip: Since the Kindle can make book browsing such a pleasure, you may also experience something that happens to me quite frequently: the desire to flag a title for possible future purchase. Naturally, Amazon has made this an easy process, with two alternative approaches available. The first is the Kindle's aforementioned **sample** feature. The second is a "Save for Later" link that you will find on the right side of each title's detail page on the Kindle. Just click there and the title will be saved under **"Save for Later" Items** accessible from the menu any time you are in the Kindle Store by way of your Kindle.

Tip: You can maintain up to 6 Kindles on the same Amazon customer account, with the same name and payment information. If you have multiple Kindle accounts you will be able to share your book purchases, but not your periodical or blog purchases, among these Kindles.

I. Updating the Latest Version of Your Kindle's Operating Software

Many of the changes and updates that Amazon will provide for the Kindle in the future will come in the form of software updates that will be sent wirelessly to your Kindle via the Whispernet. The first of these updates occurred just three months after the Kindle's launch, and for many Kindle owners the update occurred quietly before they even knew to watch for it. In any case, that update won't be the last.

If you have any concerns about whether your Kindle is running the most up-to-date version of the Kindle system software, it is easy to check. From the Kindle's Home screen, use the scroll wheel to open the "Menu" at the bottom of the screen and select "Settings." The "Settings" page will show you your Account Name, your Kindle's Device Name, any other Personal Info that you have entered (presumably for the purpose of recovering your Kindle should it be lost or stolen), your Primary Dictionary choice, the backup status of your Kindle Annotation files (enabled or disabled), and the memory status of your Kindle's native storage as well as its SD Card storage.

Also, at the bottom, of the "Settings" screen, you will find the "Version" of the software that your Kindle is running. As of August 2008, my Kindle is running Version 1.0.4.

Once you have found this information, use your computer to visit Amazon's "Updating Your Kindle Software" support page. If you were to scroll down this page ***today*** until you found the heading called "Verifying Your Software Version," you would see the following text that confirms that my Kindle is running the appropriate version:

View the version listed at the bottom of the Settings screen. The version listed should be "Kindle 1.0.4 (144750018)" or "Kindle 1.0.8 (164820023)."

If your Kindle's operating software version needs to be updated, this same Amazon support page includes instructions for triggering an update manually either wirelessly or via USB cable. If you have any difficulty carrying out these instructions, call Amazon immediately at 1-866-321-8851 (inside the U.S.) or 1-206-266-0927 (outside the U.S.). (As you may have guessed already, this is one of those instances where it makes more sense for you to follow the instructions on Amazon's own support pages rather than to follow second-hand instructions that we might include in this book).

J. Adding an SD Memory Card

Although the Kindle's native-storage capacity to hold about 200 book on a device that weighs 10.3 ounces is certainly nothing to sneeze at, many Kindle owners will want to multiply that capacity right from the get-go by picking up and installing an SD memory card.

Even if you don't expect to fill up your Kindle's native storage any time soon, installing an SD card can give you a little advantage when it comes to managing your Kindle content.

Several brands and sizes of SD memory cards are available at reasonable prices in the Kindle Store under "Accessories" and in the main Amazon store. Indeed, at this writing, prices start under $6 for a 1-gigabyte SD card that is sure to hold at least 500 additional books. Although Amazon says that SD cards up to 4 gigabytes are compatible with the Kindle, many Kindle owners have had no difficulty using SD cards up to 8 gigabytes with their Kindles.

Installation is a snap. Just remove the back cover from your Kindle and slide the SD card right into the slot provided, as shown in the little diagram right next to the slot. You're done, and the Kindle will automatically begin using the card as backup storage immediately.

Warning: Never try to remove or install an SD card on your Kindle when the Kindle's power is on.

K. How to Get Help with Your Kindle

In addition to using this book and the Kindle User's Guide, you will find plenty of helpful information on the Kindle Support website.

You can also call the Kindle Support phone numbers at 1-866-321-8851 (inside the U.S.) or 1-206-266-0927 (outside the U.S.). Telephone customer service staff are available to provide support

Monday through Friday from 6 a.m. to 8 p.m. Pacific time and weekends from 6 a.m. to 5 p.m. Pacific time.

If you wish to leave feedback or customer suggestions about the Kindle, send an email to to kindle-feedback@amazon.com.

If you want to contact me about problems you are having with your Kindle, new ideas you would like to share, or any other matter concerning this book, send an email to indieKindle@gmail.com.

L. Managing Your Kindle Content

I hesitate to say much here, because, frankly, the Kindle 1.0 content management system is such a disaster that I have been hoping since day one that Amazon would roll out a software update with significant fixes. Where are the folders, subfolders, directories, labels, something? Don't get me started, please.

So, for now, I will say four things.

First, on pages 28-33 (or locations 389-458 if you are reading it on your Kindle) of Amazon's Kindle User's Guide you will find section 2.2, Managing Your Content. Reading it will help you navigate as well as possible within a system that lacks much in the way of organizing architecture.

Second, it is a wise idea generally to **avoid using the Kindle's native Content Manager**, which is slow and clunky and makes it easier to delete content inadvertently than to do much of anything that you intend to do. (The deletions tend to occur because titles that you select for any purpose remain "selected" from one session to the next and therefore become the object of actions -- such as deleting them -- that you do not intend). You will be able to handle content management issues much more smoothly if you handle your content management needs via your computer as described in the next paragraph.

Third, Kindle owners who have installed SD cards will find it much easier and faster to ignore the Kindle's poorly named "Content Manager" altogether and, instead, to connect their Kindles to their computers via USB cable and move content around on their Kindles and their SD cards with their computers' native storage drive and folder management interfaces. While this much faster work-around will not currently allow you to create Kindle subfolders from which your Kindle can recognize and read content, you will, as one useful example, be able to organize off-Kindle content by subfolder on your SD card so that you can find it and return it to the Kindle-recognized "document" folder when you need it in the future.

Fourth, I fervently hope that, by the time you read this "page," Amazon will have introduced Kindle content management changes (and updated its documentation to explain them) that will render this a gratuitous rant by me.

IV. The Kindle's Basic Web Wireless Service: Why It Is a Revolutionary Feature, and Why Amazon Should Keep It Free

One of the more intriguing aspects of the Kindle's initial rollout in November 2007 was the degree to which Jeff Bezos and Amazon played the Kindle's most revolutionary feature so close to the vest. By marketing the Kindle as an e-book reader, Amazon kept the public focus away from the Kindle's stunning EV-DO wireless connectivity.

Why stunning?

Five main reasons:

* It allows seamless, simple same-minute delivery of any content purchased in the Kindle Store.

* It transforms the Kindle into a web-browsing computer that can access any website/

* It is fast -- essentially broadband over a cellular network.

* It is free, as compared with the $40 to $90 per month that you would pay to connect an iPhone, Blackberry or any other device to EV-DO or other wireless data services.

* The service is ubiquitous in well-populated areas, so that you never have to search for a WiFi hot spot. (Indeed, if the Kindle's popularity continues to grow, it could do serious harm to Starbucks).

So, did you get this? Did I just tell you that you could buy a mobile computer for $359 (or $259) with all of the above features, and never pay a dime to connect to the web?

Almost. That "never" remains in play, but we will come back to that.

First, let's just take pains to make this clear: the wireless connectivity, combined with the fact that the Kindle comes with its own built-in "Basic Web" browser, means that calling the Kindle an e-book reader is like calling the iPhone a cordless telephone. The Kindle is a potentially revolutionary convergence device.

To consider just how revolutionary and disruptive the Kindle could become, we should compare it briefly to three other convergence devices: the Blackberry, the iPhone and the laptop or notebook computer.

At 10.3 ounces in a package slightly smaller than a thin trade paperback, the Kindle is a little bit larger and more cumbersome than the Blackberry or the iPhone. Compared with a laptop, there is no contest. You don't need a backpack, a book bag or a briefcase to carry a Kindle. It is exactly the same as carrying a lightweight paperback book.

Both the Blackberry and the iPhone allow many people to leave their laptops at home when they leave their homes or offices. It is a bit of a toss-up. You could go either way.

But if I am carrying a Kindle when I leave my house in the morning, I cannot imagine why I would ever want to carry a laptop. Even in its small, lightweight package, the Kindle's 6-inch screen is about 3 times the size of the screens on the iPhone or other smartphones, and much easier on the eyes. If I carry a laptop, either I have to look for a WiFi hotspot or I have to pay $59.99 a month for EV-DO.

Case closed. Or open, if it is a Kindle case.

The biggest disadvantage for the Kindle, of course, is that it is not a cell phone (or is that an advantage?). It also does not make coffee. (Of course, if the Kindle 2.0 happens to show up with the capacity to connect to Skype VOIP service with that wireless connectivity – something that I acknowledge is quite unlikely -- then all bets are off).

It is interesting to speculate about why Amazon effectively did a soft launch of the free wireless "Basic Web" service while simultaneously doing a well-hyped, cover-of-Newsweek, get-Jeff-on-Charlie-Rose hard launch of the Kindle as an e-book reader. Several possible reasons come to mind:

* the desire to focus on the book-reading experience for book-reading purists who might be scared off by the potential distractions of web and web-based email connectivity

* a business need to downplay and undervalue the impact and worth of Amazon's EV-DO contract with Sprint

* business competition or regulatory issues too arcane to break down here

* the possibility that Amazon will decide at some future time to begin charging for the "Basic Web" wireless service

While a couple of these issues might be reaching a bit, each of them is interesting in its own way. Let's focus here on the issue that will have the most traction for current and future Kindle owners: the prospect that Amazon might begin assessing a monthly service fee for the wireless web. In the early blog and user-group discussions about the Kindle, there has been significant attention paid to this prospect.

It has not been lost on Kindle's early adopter users that, in its Amazon Kindle: License Agreement and Terms of Use, Amazon expressly provides for such a service fee:

> **Amazon provides wireless connectivity free of charge to you for certain content shopping and acquisition services on your Device. You will be charged a fee for wireless connectivity for your use of other wireless services on your Device, such as Web browsing and downloading of personal files, should you elect to use those services. We will maintain a list of current fees for such services in the Kindle Store. Amazon reserves the right to discontinue wireless connectivity at any time or to otherwise change the terms for wireless connectivity at any time, including, but not limited to, (a) limiting the number and size of data files that may be transferred using wireless connectivity and (b) changing the amount and terms applicable for wireless connectivity charges.**

Does that cinch it? Perhaps. Perhaps not.

The wireless service obviously has significant value. If Amazon made the service a user option with a service charge of, say, $12.95 a month, many users would pay the fee for the opportunity to use the web from nearly anywhere with such a portable, lightweight, easy-to-read device. Many others would opt out, to the fallback of using their Kindle for reading and visiting the Kindle Store -- sort of like using a Maserati as a student-driver car.

Amazon could charge for the Basic Web wireless, and there are plenty of people who believe they will, simply because they can. After all, there is no business model more popular on the Web than the perpetual monthly service charge. Compared to the wheelbarrows full of cash that Amazon will generate by selling the Kindle itself, a Kindle monthly wireless charge could generate truckloads.

Far be it from me to offer business advice to Jeff Bezos, but it says here that it would be a huge mistake for Amazon to charge anything more than a nominal fee of, say, $2.99 a month for the Basic Web wireless connectivity.

If Jeff calls and asks my advice, I will suggest $2.99 a month, because I think that a fee at that level would actually highlight the value of the service and inspire more people to check it out and use it. After all, we all deem ourselves worthy of premium-level service, don't we? All the better if we can actually afford it.

In addition to the nominal fee, it might make sense for Amazon to add on a further per-gigabyte transfer fee for individuals or business users whose usage exceeds some basic level. (One would expect that Amazon proxies all wireless traffic with the Kindle as a condition of its contract with Sprint, and thus could easily and seamlessly measure and bill for an individual's usage volume).

Why would it be a mistake for Amazon to charge a higher rate for Basic Web wireless service? Because Amazon, which understands the concept of Trojan Horse loss leaders better than any other business in the world, would lose out significantly in other important ways by pricing people out of the wireless web service:

Maximizing Kindle Unit Sales. Despite the fact that Amazon has downplayed the Basic Web wireless service, it is and will continue to be a major motivating factor behind sales of the Kindle. It will still be a major motivating factor at $2.99 a month. At $19.95 a month, not so much.

Maximizing Kindle User Time. The more that the Kindle works as a convergence device, the more its owners will use it rather than other devices. The more that Kindle owners use their Kindles as computers, the more they will buy from Amazon. (The importance of this issue, of course, would be far greater if Kindle owners were able to shop the entire Amazon store, rather than just the Kindle store, from their Kindles).

Maximizing Kindle Book Sales. The more Kindle users are on their Kindles, the more Kindle books, newspapers and articles like this one they will buy. Since it is clear that Kindle device buyers are self-identified active readers, it is likely that many or most of them could soon be buying a Kindle book per week, which will generate more revenue for Amazon than monthly services fees.

Maximizing Other Amazon Sales. It obviously behooves Amazon to make it easy and seamless for Kindle Store browsing to be linked heavily, and "sticky" with, general Amazon store browsing. Naturally, that will mean that Kindle owners who are constantly on their Kindles because of their versatility will not only be the best Kindle Store customers. They will also be the best Amazon store customers for music, video, software and hardware, and all the other countless merchandise departments at Amazon.com.

Heading Off Convergence Device Competition. As greater numbers of people realize the numerous ways in which they could use a Kindle, its greatest competition will come from the iPhone and the iPod Touch, the Blackberry, the Google phone, and laptops and handheld computers. This competition will be the primary technology competition of the remaining years of this decade. The longer Amazon keeps the Kindle wireless web free, the greater its ultimate market share. Amazon, the subject of Robert Spector's book Amazon.com: Get Big Fast, also understands the importance of dominating market share better than any business in the world. While some of these potential competitor devices may be used for eReader and other applications that allow the device owners to read books with them, Whispernet makes the Kindle the only one that offers instantaneous content delivery of over 160,000 titles.

Building the Customer Experience. Bezos has built Amazon around the idea that profit and customer loyalty follow naturally when you can provide an unparalleled customer experience in selection, price and service. Keeping the wireless service free or cheap will be a huge boost to the customer experience during the next five years, as the Kindle Book inventory grows toward Bezos' ultimate vision, that it will include every book ever printed. Amazon's market position with respect both to ereader devices and ereader content will only benefit. Conversely, many customers would see a move to milk revenue from the service as a bait-and-switch tactic, notwithstanding the fact that Amazon has already suggested such a move in its small print.

Stay tuned. As is so often true with Amazon, it will be interesting to see what's next.

But if you have an opinion about what Amazon should do with the web browser or any other services, they want to hear from you.

Make democracy work in the land of the Kindle by emailing your feedback to kindle-feedback@amazon.com.

V. How to Use the Amazon Kindle for Email: Read and answer email anywhere*, anytime on the amazing Amazon Kindle, without monthly charges

When I was a kid my mother used to buy produce off the back of a truck that came through our Jamaica Plain neighborhood each afternoon. It was fresh and inexpensive, and you found out what was available each day when the leather-lunged driver/vendor would get out of his truck calling out "Fresh tomatoes! Snap peas! Green beans! Bananas! Cantaloupes!"

Everybody on Brookley Road needed something from that list, and the guy did a good business.

Imagine if he came back to the hip, young professional neighborhood that Jamaica Plain has become today. I don't know if he would be able to sell a lot of cantaloupes. So let's give him something better suited to today's Jamaica Plain demographic: the Amazon Kindle. It would be interesting to see how he would fare.

"E-book readers!"

I don't think people would come running. Especially not at $359. JP is fairly hip, but it is still a little down-market.

"Wireless e-book readers with anywhere email!"

Okay, a few people will come out to his truck now. They may well be people who are more interested in "wireless" and "email" than "e-book reader." But a lot of other people will make an assumption about the likely asking price of that wireless service, and that assumption, however mistaken, will keep them from coming out.

As with any street vendor, this gentleman's capacity to survive depends mightily on his ability to embody a basic principle of marketing: he must translate the strengths of his product to a slogan or phrase that will connect with the desires, dreams or fears of his market so that people hear what he is calling out and say to themselves, "I want that. I need that. I cannot do without that. And I can find a way to afford that."

Sooner or later, the vendor should call out: "Read and answer email anywhere, anytime on the amazing Amazon Kindle! No monthly charges!"

Then he would get some traffic. (Three Ps: a combination of product, price-point sweet spot, and brand power).

"Hey!" you say. "What about truth in advertising?"

Well, what about it? ***It's true.***

(*Unless you live outside the U.S., or in one of those sparsely populated areas that does not yet have either of the Sprint wireless services on which the Kindle's wireless features depend).

Email on the Kindle

We can certainly speculate about all kinds of reasons why Amazon has soft-pedaled this information, but the truth is that in addition to being an e-book reader, ***the Kindle can be used, right out of the box, to read your email, send replies, and compose outgoing e-mails.***

The Kindle is not a perfect e-mail device, but it is serviceable, and very handy in a pinch when a laptop or an internet connection is not available.

It is not as multi-featured as reading e-mail on a notebook or laptop computer, but it is far more portable both in terms of weight and connectivity, since it weighs in at 10.3 ounces and does not need a WiFi signal. You can use it, and be connected with it, anywhere (*or, at least, anywhere where you could use a Sprint-enabled cellphone): on the beach, in a taxi, or just about anywhere else. In out-of-the-way places where Sprint's fast, broadband EV-DO 3G service is unavailable, there is a good chance you will be able to connect using Sprint's slower 1xRTT conventional cellular signal.

It is noticeably slower than checking email on a smartphone, so you may not want to consider this feature if you are one of these CrackBerry types who goes through 1,200 email messages a day. However, it does have two huge advantages over a smartphone.

First, its 6-inch screen is considerably more commodious and easy on the eyes than a tiny smartphone screen.

Second, let's compare the monthly charges. Smartphone data plans usually begin at $59.99 a month. The Kindle wireless web service is free. If you have a calculator on your smartphone, you can easily calculate the difference in price between these two data plans using the formula shown here: $59.99 - $0.00 = $59.99 a month savings, or $719.88 a year (yes, that is more than twice the price of a Kindle).

(By the way, there is speculation that Amazon won't keep its Whispernet wireless web service free forever. For a detailed discussion of the issues involved, read the chapter of this book entitled ***The Amazon Kindle Basic Web Wireless Service: Why It Is a Revolutionary Feature, and Why Amazon Should Keep It Free or Cheap***.

Okay, so much for comparisons. Let's get down to brass tacks.

Using Mobile Google and Gmail for Kindle Email

The key to using your Kindle device for email is provided by Google. There are other web-based email products that will work, at least sporadically, with the Kindle's web browser, but it is my belief both that none is likely over time to work better than Gmail and also that Google's commitment to a large and growing suite of mobile products is such that it makes sense for all of us as Kindle owners to engage that product suite and become its patrons and advocates sooner rather than later.

As you may be aware, Google has designed several applications for use with smartphones, cellphones and, very soon, we hear, the Google phone beta project known as the Android. These products are freely available, and you can see a list of them at the Google Mobile products page. It is quite a list. In addition to the Gmail Google email products, it includes Search, Maps, Calendar, Google Documents, a "411" telephone lookup service, SMS (also known as texting), News, Photos, Reader, Blogger, and Notebook.

If you own a Kindle or are about to own one, and you have any sense of where I am going with this, I do not blame you if you are beginning to salivate. I am far from being ready to vouch for the notion that all of these applications work seamlessly with the Kindle. Some of them are a little clunky, and one or two may not be worth using at all on Kindle 1.0. At the very least, they will take some getting used to. But these web-based software offerings can go a long way toward giving your Kindle the functionality, in a pinch, of an Internet-connected computer. As the Kindle is upgraded in coming generations, this functionality is likely to become more and more powerful.

At first blush, the idea that you can use the Kindle for email is surprising. Although Kindle comes with broadband wireless service and a basic, experimental web browser, it is impossible for a layman to install third-party software on the device (except for applications that support Kindle commercial partnerships like the one involving Audible.com). Consequently, you could never download or otherwise install email software such as Microsoft Outlook or the old AOL email environment.

That's where Google's mobile applications come in handy. Without the mobile Gmail environment, you could use the Kindle web browser to get to your Gmail account, but navigation and usefulness would be extremely limited. With the mobile Gmail account, it will still be a little slow, but you can handle all the basic tasks involved in working with your email if you follow these steps.

1. Create a Gmail account if you have not done so already. You will need to do this on your desktop or laptop computer first, by navigating to the Sign Up for Gmail page. Once you have created the account, you will be able to log in to that account on your Kindle without a hitch.

2. Get ready to access your Gmail account on your Kindle by using the scroll-wheel to navigate from the "Home" screen to the "Menu" and then selecting "Experimental." (Make sure your "Wireless" switch on the back of the Kindle is in the "on" position). Next, select "Basic Web," then use the scroll-wheel to choose Google from the "My Bookmarks" list that appears automatically on your screen. Google is included in the default listing of Bookmarks that comes fully loaded on the Kindle. You are now in the Mobile Gmail environment.

3. The first time you sign in to your Gmail account with your Kindle, you will need to use the Kindle keyboard to type in your Username and Password. After that, Gmail should take you directly to your account.

4. In your Gmail account, just use the scroll-wheel and the "Next Page" and "Prev Page" bars to move through your Inbox and read your email. It may take you a moment to rid yourself of the urge to scroll down. You can't scroll down, but you can usually accomplish the same thing by pressing the "Next Page" bar.

5. The "Inbox" of your Gmail account will present your most recent messages. Depending on the user-selectable font size you have chosen, you should be able to view 8 or 10 of these message headers at a time so that you can navigate and select easily from your Inbox. Anytime you want to check for brand new messages during a session of working with your Gmail account, just use the scroll-wheel's "Menu" selection to choose "Reload," and your screen will update with new messages within a matter of a few seconds.

6. If you need to access other areas of your Gmail account such as "Sent Mail," "Drafts," "Contact," or other Gmail features, just use the "Next Page" bar to move toward the end of your Inbox listings. You will find a listing of choices that probably include "Compose Mail," "Inbox," "Contacts," and "More." Choose the option you need or click on "More" to see further options.

7. Use the "Next Message" and/or "Next Conversation" links, as well as the "Previous" links, rather than trying to scroll down up or down, to move serially through your Inbox. The "Next conversation" link will appear at the end of the main body of text of each email message.

8. If you are using "Select" and "Next Page" to navigate among messages in your Inbox, Sent Messages, or any other Gmail label group, you can get back to the listing page by pressing once on the "Back" button or to your main Gmail page by clicking twice. The "Back" button is just below the "Next Page" bar on the right side of the Kindle.

9. To compose and send an email message, follow the process in paragraph 6 above to find "Compose Mail" on your screen, the use the "Select" wheel to choose "Compose Mail." Within seconds you will see an easy-to-use "Compose Mail" form on your screen. Easy to use in every respect, that is, except for typing with your thumbs.

10. Continue to use the "Select" wheel to choose the "To" box and populate it with one or more email addresses after you choose "Input Field." Then choose "Done." (Actually, one is plenty. You

should make sure that you've got this down cold before you start sending out "broadcast" emails).

11. Follow the same process to type in a subject line and the main text of your email. When you are finished, click on the row of buttons directly below the main text input box, then choose "Send." Even if an error message occasionally appears on your screen after you have chosen "Send," your email message has now been sent by Gmail. You can double-check on this, of course, by finding the newly sent message among your "Sent Messages."

12. You can also send replies, add "cc" and "bcc" recipients, and forward messages, using the same basic sequence of steps, by selecting "Reply," "Reply to all," or "Forward" after reading any email message in your Inbox.

13. Once you have mastered the basics of using Gmail on your Kindle, you may want try out some of the other Mobile Google features that we mentioned earlier, such as Google Calendar or the Google Reader. A great daily beginning point for Kindle users who want to get as much as possible from their Kindle web browser is a web "start page" created by Mike Elgan, author of The Book of Kindle blog. Click here to access The Kindle Start Page.

Another feature of the Google environment that can be extremely compatible with some of the more creative uses of your Kindle is called the Gmail Drive. You can use this feature to establish your own partitioned hard drive on the Google servers and access it any time through your Gmail account.

Several of these applications can make your Kindle a far more powerful device than you imagined when you first ordered it. If you can use your Kindle for receiving and sending emails, posting to your blog, maintaining calendar appointments and viewing and editing word files and spreadsheets in the Google Documents application, what exactly is this device you are holding in your hand? An e-book reader? Or a computer?

It is both. It is clearly designed to be an e-book reader, and while few glitches remain to be ironed out (how hard can it be to add some Velcro to the cover and to shorten the length of the next-page buttons by half?), it rates high in ease of use as an e-book reader. As I have suggested, it is a tad clunky as a computer, but the price, versatility and portability can make up for a lot of clunkiness -- and all of a sudden that $359 price tag seems like a bargain.

It will be interesting to see how quickly or flexibly Amazon provides updates or Kindle 2.0 versions to make it easier to use these and other applications. Being a manufacturer has not heretofore been part of Amazon's DNA, although the Kindle in general is not a bad beginning. It seems far more likely during the next couple of years that Google will alter its mobile applications to accommodate the Kindle than that Amazon will do much to rejigger the Kindle web browser itself. Naturally, there will also be a lot of programming done by creative independent geniuses and other third-party folks.

I should add a note here regarding the slowness of using the Kindle for email. Although, as I said, the actual process of navigating among your emails is slower than it is on a laptop, the convenient fact that your broadband service is always there, and comes on with a flip of the switch, helps to offset that lack of speed. You'll never have to sit in a Starbucks for five minutes trying to figure out how to find a hot spot or otherwise connect to a WiFi signal. Matter of fact, you'll never even have to find a Starbucks unless, like me, you are susceptible to getting a Jones for that Starbucks coffee.

Emailing Content to Your Kindle Address

There's one more very cool email-related feature of the Kindle that is well worth mentioning here, in part so that you do not confuse it with the web-base Gmail service that have been discussing. We recommend, obviously, that you use Gmail for web-based email. In addition, Amazon provides your Kindle with its own email address and uses that address to send you any files that you send to Amazon for conversion into Kindle-friendly files. (You first have to approve the transmitting email address using your "Manage Your Kindle" page on your Amazon account page, from your computer).

Amazon initially announced that it would charge 10 cents per document to email you these Kindle-compatible files, but appears never to have charged anyone the dime and, at least for now, appears to have dropped the charge entirely. Amazon will convert any document you send in Word, PRC, HTML, TXT, JPEG, GIF, PNG or BMP format, and has also done very well with .pdf documents that I have sent for conversion. Just to be clear, that means you can download the complete file of Moby Dick from Project Gutenberg, send it to your Kindle email account that Amazon has provided, and

Amazon will zap it to you as a Kindle document at no charge. (If you are out of wireless range -- in Montana or outside the country, for instance -- you can also send the document to a slightly different form of your Kindle email address [johndoe@free.kindle.com rather than johndoe@kindle.com] and Amazon will send it to your PC so that you can use your USB cable to transfer it to your Kindle).

You can also receive documents that others email to your kindle.com address, but only if you go to your Manage Your Kindle page on your Amazon account and approve the sender in advance.

Troubleshooting Tips if You Have Difficulty Accessing Gmail or Other Web Pages

If you have trouble accessing your Gmail account, another Kindle-compatible webmail account, or any website that is not too graphics-intensive to load onto the Kindle's display, here are a few troubleshooting tips that you may want to try:

* Go to your Kindle web browser "Settings" page (using the menu option from within the browser). Set "View Mode" to Advanced, and select "Enable" for JavaScript.

* It is a good idea every now and then, on that same Settings page, to clear your History and your Cache, which will help protect you against freeze-ups, etc. The trade-off, which you will also experience when you reset your Kindle or disconnect and reconnect its battery, is that you will also have to get your thumbs working to type in your user ID and password anew for Gmail and any other websites that require you to log in.

* Just in case your difficulty springs from the URL with which you are entering Gmail, try typing this URL into the URL input field:

m.google.com

or

http://m.google.com

That URL should bring you to a list of the mobile Google products, from which you can select Gmail and be delivered quickly to a Gmail sign-in page.

* Finally -- and I would be more hesitant to suggest the following if I hadn't done this myself more than once -- double check your user ID and password for the website on your computer and make sure they work there, just to make sure you haven’t changed them and forgotten about the new ones. Then try them again on your pesky Kindle keyboard.

Good luck!

VI. Using Google Reader to Read Your Favorite Blogs on the Kindle

For many Kindle owners, the Kindle is all about convenience, and there is nothing at all wrong with that. When it comes to reading blogs on the Kindle, you may be perfectly content to pay a monthly fee for the experience. You may even be satisfied with Amazon's selection of (at this writing) 424 blogs from which you may choose (up from about 300 at launch, but still a tiny and rather corporate selection from among the millions of fascinating blogs now available on the web). If you're satisfied, you need not read further in this particular chapter of ***The Complete User's Guide to the Amazing Amazon Kindle***.

But if you are the kind of independent-minded reader who prefers to **make your own selections**, there is another way. If you prefer not to be charged money for content that is intended by its authors to be available **free of charge**, yes, there is another way.

By following the few, very easy steps outlined in this chapter, you can adapt Google Reader to your Kindle so that it fetches the blog content that you are most interested in reading and pushes that content right to your Kindle's web browser where you may read it anywhere, anytime, and at absolutely no cost.

What is Google Reader?

Google Reader is yet another nifty web-based service from Google. It aggregates content through RSS feeds from the web, based on each individual's tastes and selections and serves the content in real time to an individual's personal Google Reader page for reading on- or off-line. It is compatible through web browser platforms with a wide variety of devices, including the Kindle. For a delightfully simple, elegant, and useful 3-minute video explanation of Google Reader in plain English, check out the CommonCraft video at http://www.commoncraft.com/rss_plain_english.

Set Up Your Google Accounts

The first step, if you haven't already taken care of this, is to establish a Google account. As you follow various suggestions in this book for making the most of your Kindle, it is very likely that you will be using several features of your Google account including Google Reader, Gmail, Google Blog Search, Google Search, Google Notebook, Google Calendar, Blogger, and Google News. Although we are still only about 9 months into the Age of the Kindle, it is becoming increasingly clear that, whether or not Google and Amazon ever enter into any explicit joint agreements regarding services that optimize the Kindle, Google will be a steady source for useful enhancements for Kindle owners.

All of Google's services can be accessed through a single Google user account. For most people, the most convenient approach will be to use the same Google account with your Kindle that you use on your desktop or notebook computer. However, there may be some circumstances in which it is useful to employ separate accounts for different devices. For instance, if you use Google Reader to follow multimedia-intensive blogs on your computer, you may want to use a separate account for subscriptions to the more text-intensive blogs that are suitable for Kindle reading.

Bookmark Your Google Mobile And Google Reader Pages

Creating bookmarks for Google Reader and other mobile Google services in your Kindle's web browser will save you and your thumbs a lot of extra work in the future, and it is an easy process.

1. Use the switch on the back of your Kindle to turn on the Kindle's wireless feature.

2. From your Kindle's "Home" screen, use the scroll wheel to select and click on "Menu" at the bottom of the screen.

3. Select "Experimental" from the menu selections, and then choose "Basic Web" from the "Experimental" page.

4. Use the Kindle's scroll wheel to select "Menu" at the bottom of the screen and click on "Settings" from the menu selection. On the web browser's Settings page, enable (or verify that you have already enabled) "Advanced" Mode (rather than "Default" Mode and Javascript. (Note: the web browser's Settings page is different from the Settings page accessible directly from your Kindle's "Home" screen.)

5. Click on "Enter URL" at the top of the next screen and type the following into the input field to the right of the "http://" prefix:

m.google.com

6. When the Google Mobile products page loads onto your Kindle screen, use the Kindle's scroll wheel to select "Menu" at the bottom of the screen and click on "Add Bookmark" from the menu selection.

7. From the Google Mobile products page, use the Kindle's scroll wheel to select "Reader" from the Google Mobile products choices.

8. When the Google Reader page loads onto your Kindle screen, use the Kindle's scroll wheel to select "Menu" at the bottom of the screen and click on "Add Bookmark" from the menu selection.

You will then have bookmarks for the top-level Google Mobile products page and for the Google Reader page. You may, of course, follow similar steps to bookmark other Google pages that you expect to use.

How to Subscribe to Your Favorite Blogs With Google Reader

Generally speaking, you will find it much easier to use your computer, rather than your Kindle, to search out your favorite blogs and add them to your Google Reader subscriptions so that you can then have easier access to them on your Kindle. It is an easy process:

1. Find a blog that you want to add to your Google Reader subscriptions. Find the RSS Feed button on the blog and copy it. (In many cases, you can simply type the blog's URL into the input field rather than looking for an RSS Feed button).

2. Open the main Google Reader page. The shortest URL that I have found for this is reader.google.com. If you haven't already signed in with your Google account, do so.

3. From the "sidebar" column to the left of your Google Reader screen, select the **Add Subscriptions** link.

4. Copy the RSS feed link of the blog to which you want to subscribe into the input field that opens when you select the **Add Subscriptions** link. The blog will now be included in your Google Reader subscriptions. (As noted above, in many cases, you can simply type the blog's URL into the input field rather than looking for an RSS Feed button).

How to Read Blogs on the Kindle with Google Reader

Once you have attended to the steps above, reading blogs on the Kindle is remarkably simple and user-friendly.

1. Use the switch on the back of your Kindle to turn on the Kindle's wireless feature.

2. From your Kindle's "Home" screen, use the scroll wheel to select and click on "Menu" at the bottom of the screen.

3. Select "Experimental" from the menu selections, and then choose "Basic Web" from the "Experimental" page.

4. Choose "Google Reader" from your Kindle web browser's bookmarks (the bookmark is there because you followed the steps in an earlier section to create it). The Bookmarks page is the "default" page that usually appears first when you enter the web browser, but if another page comes up instead, just use the scroll wheel to click on "Menu" at the bottom of the screen and select "Bookmarks."

5. When the "Google Reader" page loads to your Kindle screen, you may be required to provide the log-in name and password of your Google account, but generally you will only be required to do this when your browser's cache has been cleared either manually or by a system re-set. Once you log in, you are ready to start reading.

6. In order to "sort" your blogs and read only the posts on a particular blog, just click on "Subscriptions" from the "Google Reader" page and select the blog you wish to read. Generally, this will create a more pleasurable reading experience than jumping from

one subject matter to another, and it will also come in handy as a way of protecting you from losing track of the content on a two-posts-per-day blog that might otherwise be overwhelmed by posts from other blogs if you have subscribed to news site blogs or other prolific posters.

Selecting Kindle Blogs from the Kindle Store

I should know better than to tamper with the revenue streams for the Kindle and the Amazon website. After all, to paraphrase the "Chico Escuela" line for which Garret Morris' Saturday Night Live character will always be remembered, the Kindle "has been berry, berry good to me." So I am going to hazard the possibility that I might be called an Amazon shill and take a moment here to point out that it is also extremely convenient, and relatively inexpensive, to subscribe to any of the Kindle Store's blog offerings directly through your Kindle.

The blog subscriptions that are available in the Kindle Store are pushed directly to your Kindle without any advertising or any other revenue-producing architecture other than the relatively nominal monthly subscription charges, which provide an economic incentive for their authors and publishers to make this content available directly on the Kindle.

To make selections from these offerings, just navigate to the Kindle Home Page and select Kindle Store Bestsellers: Blogs Only (the url, if you are using your computer, is http://amazon.com/gp/bestsellers/digital-text/241647011/ebest). Select any blog that interests you and it will start downloading to your Kindle whenever there is new content. In most cases, the Kindle Store offers you a free two-week trial before it begins charging you a nominal monthly rate -- usually $0.99 to $1.99 per month).

VII. Traveling with Your Kindle

As you may have heard, the Kindle is only available for sale "officially" in the United States as of this writing in August 2008, and certain features such as those that rely directly and exclusively on the Kindle's Whispernet wireless connectivity are only intended to work within the United States. In spite of these limitations, the Kindle is nonetheless one of the greatest travel accessories ever invented. Please, don't leave home without it.

Instead of carrying heavy bags full of books on your business trip or vacation, the Kindle will allow you to carry hundreds of books with you in a 10.3-ounce package, or thousands if you make an extremely worthwhile investment in an SD memory card. Your Kindle will provide you with all the reading content that you download to it, but that's not all.

You will also want to bring your laptop computer and the USB cable that comes with your Kindle. Connect your Kindle to the laptop, log on to the Internet anywhere in the world, and you will be able to get your daily newspapers and purchase and download new books, articles, blogs, and magazines. Naturally, you will have to use a credit card with a U.S. address to make all your Kindle content purchases (as with your purchase of the Kindle itself) since the content currently available in the Kindle store is, by and large, content for which Amazon owns the U.S. selling rights.

Here are a few additional tips to enhance your enjoyment of your Kindle and its remarkable functionality when you are on the road.

Using the Kindle to Translate Foreign or Technical Words and Phrases

Much has been made of the fact that the Kindle, as of this writing, is not yet available outside the United States, and that some of its appealing features -- all of those that depend on a wireless connection -- are useless when a Kindle owner lives or is traveling outside the United States or, for that matter, in a Sprint wireless dead zone. However, there are a surprising number of ways in which a Kindle can come in handy when you are on the road, and here is another. This one is helpful if you are traveling in a land where you do not speak the native language.

Before your trip to France, for instance, buy a Kindle edition of a good French-English/English-French dictionary and, of course, download it to your Kindle. Then, all you have to do is click on the "SEARCH" key on the bottom row of your Kindle keyboard, type any word or phrase into the input field, and use the scroll-wheel to select "Go." Presto, your Kindle will search its onboard content for the word or phrase. By selecting and clicking on an iteration of the word or phrase from your bilingual dictionary, you should be looking at the translation that you need in a few seconds. It won't be lightning fast, but it should be serviceable.

By using the same principle and the appropriate reference material, of course, the Kindle can also be used to render professional and technical language and terms. As with any search function, your ability to make effective use of the Kindle's translation powers is bound to improve with use and familiarity.

Making the Most of Your Kindle Connections Overseas or in a Sprint Wireless Dead Zone

There are myriad reasons why you'll want to take your Kindle on your next trip to a foreign land. Before you go, you'll be able to download many of the books that you might otherwise have to lug with you. And while it is true that you probably won't be able to do any more direct wireless downloading during your trip, that need not keep you from making extensive use of your Kindle.

To make the most of your Kindle overseas, bring your Kindle's USB cable, your laptop, and -- if you have one -- a Blackberry or other smartphone. In each place where you hang your hat, you will want to find the best internet connection available -- for these purposes, "best" means fast, accessible, and cheap or free. Just because a city that you are visiting has a Starbucks or some other well-known Internet café does not mean that's your best source of Internet access. Technology culture blogger Mike Elgan has written of finding that Starbucks in Greece was charging $660 per month for Internet access, only to discover that "right next door is a better coffee joint where a month of Wi-Fi costs you zero." If you are staying somewhere more than a day or two, a little research to find the "best" connection available should be well worth the time. To find Internet coverage while you are traveling inside or outside the U.S., www.jiwire.com is a helpful resource. To check on Kindle wireless coverage areas, just navigate to http://www.showmycoverage.com/IMPACT.jsp and enter zip codes or other information to see mapping of Sprint wireless coverage areas anywhere in the United States.

With a daily downloading blast to your computer followed by a USB transfer to your Kindle, you will easily be able to use your Kindle to keep up with books, newspaper and magazine subscriptions, blogs and other content and read them offline at your leisure during your trip. Just log in to your Amazon account and have your content sent to your computer via the Internet. If you need to receive documents, manuscripts, memoranda, or PDF files while you are abroad, just have them sent to your youraddress@free.kindle.com email address and you can transfer them to your Kindle each morning (or any other time of day) with ease.

In a pinch, if you have a smartphone data plan like the AT&T Unlimited Domestic and International Data Plan, you might even be able to tether your laptop to a Blackberry or other device. The economics of such a solution are compelling; the only problem is that tethering appears to be outlawed under such a plan.

Using the Kindle as a Travel Guide

Whether you are exploring the wonders of your own city or state or traveling around the world, the Kindle can help you get more out of a travel guide than you ever thought possible. The first step, of course, is to purchase and download the travel guides and reference materials that you want for your trip before you leave.

Once this content is "on board" your Kindle, you can search and retrieve material from it, without any wireless or other connection, simply by using the Kindle's powerful local search feature. Technology culture writer and blogger Mike Elgan wrote recently of using Kindle search to learn everything he needed to know in order to maximize his appreciation and understanding of ancient Greek ruins such as the Temple of Poseidon while en route to the sites.

Once you've got good reference material on your Kindle, all you have to do is click on the "SEARCH" key on the bottom row of your

Kindle keyboard, type any word or phrase into the input field, and use the scroll-wheel to select "Go." Presto, your Kindle will search its onboard content for the word or phrase. By selecting and clicking on a reference from your travel material, you can be reading up on any topic within in a moment or two.

The Kindle and GPS - Intriguing but Frustrating

Okay, let's not get carried away here. I've listed several GPS commands in the "shortcuts" section of this book, and the idea that the Kindle comes with any built-in GPS functionality is such a cool notion that it is easy to overstate what you can do with it. My general warning is that if you are going to depend upon your Kindle's GPS to help you navigate while mobile, there is a fair chance you will end up lost. The main reason for this is that the device relies on Google Maps for its GPS-like services, and Google Maps is not visually optimized for the Kindle. If you've ever switched to a larger font while reading content on the Kindle, there is a good chance that you will be frustrated trying to read street names on the Kindle's representation of a Google street map. I've also found that Google Maps often does not "read" the address information that the Kindle transmits regarding its location, so that if, for instance, I am using the Alt-3 command to find a nearby restaurant, I have to delete the data that my Kindle has transmitted to Google Maps and replace it with a street address, zip code, or both.

That being said, these features represent some tentative baby steps in a pretty cool direction -- not to mix metaphors. Once you are in the Kindle's Web Browser, clicking on Alt-1 will provide a Google Maps representation of your current location. Alt-2 will help you find nearby gas stations, and Alt-3 nearby restaurants. I am anticipating more fun, and a better viewing experience, with Kindle 2.0 or 3.0.

Checking Sprint Wireless Coverage for the Kindle

Just navigate to http://www.showmycoverage.com/IMPACT.jsp and enter zip codes or other information to see mapping of Sprint wireless coverage areas anywhere in the United States. To find Internet coverage while you are traveling inside or outside the U.S., www.jiwire.com is a helpful resource.

Downloading Kindle Editions Via USB Cable

Being outside the Kindle's wireless service area, or even outside the United States, need not be an obstacle to getting Kindle edition books, newspapers and other content quickly, as long as you have a computer with Internet access and an Amazon account, linked to your Kindle, with a U.S. credit card as the registered form of payment. In addition to your Kindle and a connected computer, the other piece of hardware that is essential for this operation, of course, is the USB cable that comes in the box with the Kindle. (Note: this is a device-specific USB cable rather than a cable with standard USB connections at both ends, although I was happy to find during a recent crisis of disorganization that the device-specific USB cable that had come with an old Creative Zen MP3 player a few years back was a perfect fit for the Kindle).

The process is simple and straightforward. Just log on to your Amazon account on your computer, go to the title's Kindle Edition detail page, and purchase the book, newspaper, magazine, or blog. Naturally, it will not show up immediately on your Kindle, since the Kindle is not connected wirelessly via the Whispernet.

Your next move, therefore, will be to navigate to to Your Media Library in your Amazon account, click on the "Downloads" tab from the choices across the top and choose Kindle books, newspapers, magazines, blogs, music and other audio files, and Audible.com files from the selections on the "Downloads" pull-down menu. You may sort your downloads either by title or by purchase date. Then just choose the title you want to download from those you have already purchased, and select the "Download to computer" button at the right, just below the "No wireless coverage?" prompt. As the download occurs, make a note of the download location on your computer so that you will be able to find the download easily for the next step.

Once your download has occurred, make sure that your Kindle is in "on" and "awake" mode, and connect the Kindle to your Kindle via the USB cable. Then just transfer the new Kindle content from your computer to your Kindle or your Kindle's SD card (if you have one). Be sure to place reading content in your Kindle's "documents" folder, Audible.com files (.aa) in the "audible" folder, and other audio content in the music folder.

Once you have made this transfer, disconnect your Kindle from your computer and -- perhaps after a few seconds while you see an "Updating" message at the bottom of the Kindle screen -- you will be able to read the new content on your Kindle.

If the content that you wish to transfer to your Kindle is in the form of subscription content for a newspaper, magazine, or blog, you will of course have to repeat this process for each daily, weekly, or monthly transmission of content. With subscription content, the "Your Media Library" page for your Amazon account will provide an individual download option for each "issue" that you might wish to download. However, be aware, for instance, that with daily issues of a newspaper, these issues will only be available to you for direct download from Amazon for a period of one week. However, you may keep them as long as you wish on your Kindle or on your SD card.

VIII. The Kindle as a Writing, Editing, and Publishing Device

Taking Notes on the Kindle - It's All in the Thumbs.

If you can teach your thumbs to type, there are several effective ways to take notes on the Kindle for future use and editing. You could write an entire novel on the Kindle, although you would likely run into two problems along the way. First, you would have to break it into smaller documents so as not to be working with too large a document size for the Kindle's memory. Second, you just wouldn't. Would you? But here are several useful ways to make notes on the Kindle, depending on your situation and objectives.

Annotation within a Kindle Document. If you move the silvery cursor to any line on any page of a Kindle document and click on the scroll wheel, a choice of three interactive selections will appear on your screen: "Lookup," " Add Highlight," and "Add Note." By clicking on the "Add Note" selection you can type in text and save it in a "My Clippings" file for later retrieval through your computer, which will recognize the Kindle as, for instance, an E: or F: drive with folders for your notes, marks, and clippings. Your aggregate "My Clippings" file will appear as if it were an e-book or any other title with your Kindle content on your Home screen and as a text file in your Kindle's "documents" folder when the Kindle is connected to your computer via USB cable.

Google Notebook. This feature is present in the same Google Mobile features menu that includes Gmail and Google Reader. With Google Notebook you will find it easy to maintain and save multiple notebook documents and move seamlessly back and forth between your Kindle and your computer in writing, editing, and annotating these documents, with no need for downloading or USB transfers.

Annotating Your Working Documents. You can email any document (.doc, .txt, .pdf, for instance) to your Kindle address (<you>@kindle.com) and use the aforementioned annotation process to continue working on it while using your Kindle. Just so your expectations of synchronicity don't get the better of you here, it is worth mentioning that you won't be able to transmit an annotated file from your Kindle back to your computer as a single document. You'll have to transfer the annotations separately.

Writing and Annotation to Email. At the risk of overburdening the idea a "work around," I'll mention that opening a "compose email" window through your Kindle's web browser, typing, and sending it back to your email address can be a convenient way of making, saving, and revisiting notes on your Kindle, with the benefit of creating a file that you can access from anywhere.

Saving, Printing, Editing and Working with Your Kindle Clippings, Annotations, and Highlighted Text. Once you enable "Backup of Annotations" on your Kindle's main "Settings" page (which you select from the Menu at the bottom of your Home screen), you will find it astonishingly easy to save, print, edit, and work with text that you annotate, clip or highlight with your Kindle. The Kindle will automatically save your annotations, clippings, and highlighted text in a document called "My Clippings," which will appear on your Home screen so that you can open it and read it just as you would read any other book or document on your Kindle.

Then, when you connect your Kindle via USB cable with your computer, you will find your "My Clippings" file in **.txt** format within the Kindle's "Documents" folder. Open it as you would open any text file on your computer and you will be able to save, edit, cut and paste, print or work with it or parts of it in any way that you please. You can even email it to colleagues, friends, family, or other members of your reading group.

Once you begin making annotations, bookmarks, etc., within a document, the pull-up Menu at the bottom of the screen from anywhere within that document will allow you to select "My Notes and Marks," from which you can read the notes you have already made.

Tip: Since the Kindle can capture only one single display-screen "page" at a time for the purposes described in this section, you may want to adjust your font size to the smallest font available when you are using these features so as to maximize your access to text.

20 Steps to Publishing a Kindle Edition of Your Book or Document: How to Use Kindle, Amazon and the Web to Market Your Book and Connect with Readers

Anyone can publish Kindle editions of books, articles or other documents for which he owns the publishing rights. You set your own price for the Kindle edition at the time of publication, and Amazon pays you 35% of the proceeds for electronic copies sold in each calendar month about 60 days after the close of the month. As I write this, the allowable range in which you may set a Kindle edition price ranges from 99 cents up to $199.99.

However, it would be shortsighted to see that revenue or royalty as the main or only reason to publish a Kindle edition. Getting your work out there in Kindle form may help build readership for all your writing efforts during this time of publishing-industry transition. In time, of course, it could also lead to significant Kindle revenue.

While it is natural to think first of writers of a creative bent who will now be able to bring out their works of fiction, memoir, narrative or inspirational nonfiction, poetry, and other forms to connect with specific groups of interested readers, the Kindle is also very likely to provide an important platform for entrepreneurial authors with particular notions about how to use the e-books and articles of various lengths to provide information and market their services, products, brands, and companies.

Publishing a Kindle edition of your book or document is both free and relatively easy, but as with everything else you do as a writer, it is important to do things the right way from the start. Once you put your writing out there on the Web, it is likely to remain out there permanently, even if you attempt to pull it back.

Getting things right for the Kindle applies, of course, to the usual processes of manuscript preparation and your insistence on excellence. Equally important, however, are the initial processes of setting up your Kindle Edition in ways that will help you and Amazon to market your book or document effectively over the long haul. Items that need special care here include choosing a title and subtitle, selecting the content categories under which your title will be listed, writing a description of the title, setting a retail price and establishing the search keywords under which your title will be searchable in Amazon's Kindle inventory and, ultimately, elsewhere on the web as well.

Because these things are so critically important to your success as a Kindle author, it is essential that you prepare off-line for the process of following the steps below. Open a word processing file (or get out a yellow legal pad, if you prefer), and go through the publishing steps to prepare the content that you will use before you post it. This content will very likely be some of the most important marketing content you ever write for your Kindle edition, so it is well worth a little extra time.

You shouldn't compose your search keyword lists on the Amazon screens any more than you should write a novel on the Amazon screens. In addition to the fact that drafting this material off-line will allow you to edit, revise and improve it, it also carries the extra benefit of allowing you to save the material in document form so that you can use it again or get it back if you somehow lose your Internet connection or your place in the process midstream. So, just to be clear, let me repeat that my suggestion is that you go through the following 20 steps in draft form before actually entering material on Amazon's website.

1. ***Make a Publication Decision***. Begin by deciding what you are going to publish. If you are publishing an entire book, then this is an obvious and easy decision. But don't overlook the potential for publishing articles and book excerpts as short-form documents in Kindle editions. If you are a non-fiction author or publisher, see if there are chapters that you can excerpt and price at $1.99 or so. These may not make you a lot of money, but if the content is good they may help you to connect with readers and market your books as well as other articles. Short-form documents are ideal for Kindle, and in our ultra-searchable information society they can help you to build a platform and a higher profile in the Kindle Store and beyond. **One important tip: in everything you publish as a Kindle edition, include easy-to-find links to a common website, blog, or a page where readers can find a linked bibliography of all your publications.**

2. ***Manuscript Preparation***. Prepare your manuscript in a single file document for Kindle edition publication. Your may prepare the document in any format that is supported by Amazon's Digital Text Platform, including Microsoft Word (.doc), PDF (.pdf), Plain Text (.txt), HTML (.html or .htm), Zipped HTML (.zip) or Mobi (.mobi or .prc). With simple text documents, there is no need to transfer or save the file as a PDF or HTML file, since Amazon's Digital Text Platform will take care of all the formatting and give you the

opportunity to preview it before you publish your Kindle Edition. With documents that include artwork or other embedded files, use a format that will fix the embedded files properly within your overall document. The ideal format for successful content conversion by Amazon's Digital Text Platform appears to occur with a Microsoft Word document that has been saved with the "Save as HTML" command, following this recommendation from Amazon: ***"Amazon DTP provides support for Microsoft Word .doc files. We recommend that you use 'Save As HTML' (in a filtered or simplified format, if available) [to save] your documents before uploading them. However, standard .doc files will often convert without a hitch."***

3. ***Front Matter***. Create a brief title and copyright page at the beginning of your document, if it is not already there. This page should begin with the full title and the author's full name. Below that should appear the name, city, website address and email address of the publishing company, if any, followed by two lines such as this:

First Kindle Original Edition, December 2007

Copyright 2007 by Stephen Windwalker

Finally, add the following paragraph, unless you are publishing material that you intend for the public domain:

All rights reserved. This book may not be reproduced in any form, in whole or in part (beyond that copying permitted by U.S. Copyright Law, Section 107, "fair use" in teaching or research, Section 108, certain library copying, or in published media by reviewers in limited excerpts), without written permission from the publisher.

You may wish to remove pagination from your Table of Contents and Index, since page numbers are not steadfast in Kindle documents due, among other things, to the fact that the Kindle allows a reader to change the font size in any document.

4. ***Hyperlinks in Your Text***. If your book or document is non-fiction, consider embedding links within the document to allow Kindle readers to navigate to other websites using the wireless "Basic Web" functionality that comes with the Kindle.

5. ***Digital Text Platform***. Go to Amazon's Digital Text Platform website at http://dtp.amazon.com/mn/signin. You will see a "Welcome to Digital Text Platform - amazon.com" banner across the

top of the page. On the left is a sign-in box where you can log on with your Amazon email address and password. You will also find links to "help" and "community forum" pages, which I suggest that you bookmark immediately under a "Kindle" label or folder.

6. ***Sign In***. Sign in using your Amazon.com account, or establish a new account with a separate email address if you want to keep your Kindle edition publishing activity distinct both from your other Amazon activity and from other household members who may share your Amazon or email account. Make sure you keep track, in a secure place, of the email address and password that you establish for Amazon's Digital Text Platform. Few things are more frustrating than establishing such an account and then not being able to access it.

7. ***Enter Account Information***. Click on "My Account" to provide the important information that Amazon must have to pay your share of the proceeds from the sale of electronic copies of your Kindle Edition. Provide a full, official name for yourself or your company, depending on who owns the rights to the books or other documents that you will publish on Kindle. Type in a postal mailing address, select the business type from the pull-down menu, and enter the information for the bank account into which Amazon will electronically deposit your payments. You must have both the account number and the bank routing number to proceed here.

8. ***Add New Item***. Using the navigation tabs at the top of the Digital Text Platform screen, click on "My Shelf," then "Add New Item." The first screen you will see is headed "Enter Product Details," and it is here that you enter the most important "marketing" material that will help Kindle owners and others search for and find your books and articles.

9. ***ISBN for Linking to Other Editions***. You do not need an ISBN to publish a Kindle edition. However, if your book or article has a hard-copy version with an ISBN, you can type or paste the 10-digit version of it, with or without hyphens, in the ISBN box. This will enable Amazon to create a linked connection between the Kindle, hardcover, paperback and other versions of your document, which will help to enhance your sales. Keep it mind that Kindle owners are not the only people who will search for Kindle editions. Because of the high level of buzz concerning the Kindle, millions of other Amazon customers will scout for Kindle edition titles. In some cases this will lead them back to the dead-tree versions of these titles,

and in other cases they will decide, on the basis of the growing Kindle selection, that it is time to get Kindles of their own. If there is no version of your title with an ISBN, just skip the ISBN field.

10. ***Titles and Subtitles***. Enter the full title and subtitle of your book or article in the Title field, with proper capitalization and a colon after the title, as in this example: **20 Steps to Publishing a Kindle Edition of Your Book or Document: How to Use Kindle, Amazon and the Web to Market Your Book and Connect with Readers.** Yes, that's a mouthful. But that can be a good thing -- not the fact that it is a long title, but the fact that it is a logical, informative title that is dense with searchable words. Subtitles are more important than ever in publishing, because when they are optimized for web searching in general, and Amazon searching specifically, they can help take advantage of the marketing power of a website like Amazon's. Note also that, because it starts with a number, the article title is also optimized for alphabetical listings.

11. ***Description***. Write a professional, attractive description of your document, with copy similar to what might appear on a back cover or inside dustjacket flap. Proofread it carefully and paste it into the "Description" field. Don't exaggerate, embellish or make false claims about the document, or disappointed readers will be sure to retaliate with negative reviews. If the article is excerpted from a longer book, mention the book. Include a one-liner from a review if it would be helpful, with accurate quoting and attribution, of course. A brief biographical sketch of the author may also be appropriate. Amazon will force you to be succinct, since the Description field is limited to 850 characters, or about 175 words.

12. ***Publisher, Language and Pub Date***. Enter the name of the document's publisher in the "Publisher" field. This may be either an individual or a publishing company. However, if you are approaching this question for the first time, give it some thought. If you are publishing content that requires or deserves some gravitas, calling your publishing company "Jack's Publishing" may not help. You may also want to consider using your publishing company's URL in this field, as an easy way to lure prospective readers to a website or blog where you can list other titles and provide more information.

Enter the language in which your content appears under "Language" and the publication date under "Pub Date." If your content has been published elsewhere previously, enter the original publication date. With nonfiction this is a matter, among other things, of truth in advertising, because some non-fiction work can obviously become outdated over time. If your work is appearing for the first time, the Kindle Store will automatically enter the date the item is being published once everything has been processed.

13. ***Content Categories***. Carefully select the Kindle content categories that Amazon will use to help readers find your content. Category headings such as these are different from keywords that you invent for your title. You are only allowed 5 categories, and they must all come from Amazon's tree structure of category and subcategory headings. When you see a plus sign next to a category, you can click on it to find subcategories. Study the choices and try to imagine the categories that your readers would be most likely to use if they were hunting for a book or article like yours. Don't try to trick the system, but do be open to spreading the field a bit by thinking about different types of appeal that your article might have. For instance, the keywords for this article might include "Writing" as well as "Marketing," two categories that appear in different areas of the category tree structure.

14. ***Contributors***. Under "Authors," enter the names of the people who contributed to your content, including authors, editors, illustrators, translators, and individuals who wrote an introduction or preface. Although this may seem straightforward, one thing that is often overlooked is the importance of entering an author's name ***exactly*** as it may appear elsewhere in Amazon's catalogue. Since Amazon automatically hyperlinks author names, this consistency is essential if you want to make it easy for readers to find multiple works by the same author.

15. ***Search Keywords***. The importance of what you enter in the field called "Search Keywords" cannot be overstated, so take the time to prepare well and get the most out of this. As you are certainly aware, Amazon's success as an online bookseller owes much to its success in making it easy for customers to search for the content they want, and to view Amazon's suggestions for items they may want based on past purchases, on the Amazon website. There are thousands of web marketing experts whose primary activity is to optimize web pages for search engines from Amazon's to Google's to many others so that web browsers, surfers and seekers will be able to find specific clients' products, content and activities on the web. Amazon's ability to generate sales for the content you post for Kindle

depends mightily on your success at entering the most suitable keywords in the "Search Keywords" field.

The key to successful search keyword selection lies in your ability to zero in on the overlapping "sweet spot" at the intersection of two imaginary circles. In one circle, imagine words and very short phrases that would be likely choices to direct searchers to your book, article or other content. In a second circle, imagine the most popular and effective search keywords that people enter to find content on the Amazon website. Where the two circles overlap, you have search words that stand a reasonable chance of actually bringing significant traffic to your content.

As you have probably already guessed, there are entire books on this process. Amazon's recommendation is that you select 5 to 7 individual words or very short phrases to populate the "Search Keywords" field. To help develop your understanding of how the process works, experiment with the Google Adwords Keyword Tool online at https://adwords.google.com/select/KeywordToolExternal. Additionally, check for new resources and services at the Independent Publishing with Kindle Books website at http://indiekindle.blogspot.com/.

16. ***Other Bibliographic Information***. Populate the fields for "Edition Number," "Series Title," and "Volume Number." Amazon's instructions for edition number are to enter a simple number, e.g., "1," to denote whether this is the first published version of your content or a revised version. A series title might refer either to the serial name, such as "A Series of Unfortunate Events," or to an imprint title denoting a specific thematic preoccupation, such as "Harvard Perspectives in Entrepreneurship." Volume numbers are intended for magazines, journals or full-length works in a series.

17. ***Product Image***. Upload an appropriate cover image in the "Product Image" field. A cover image of a hard-copy edition of your work is suitable here, and can help generate interest in your content just as covers attract browsers in bookstores. Your product image must be in TIFF (.tif/.tiff) or JPEG (.jpeg/.jpg) format, and must be at least 500 pixels on the longest side. If you do not have a hard-copy edition of your book, it may be worthwhile to design and digitize a product image so that you can upload it here to enhance the browsing experience. It is not strictly necessary, however, and you may also add an image at any time after you have published your content as a Kindle edition.

18. ***Save or Change Product Details***. As you are following each of the above steps it is helpful to click on the "Save Entries" button after each step. This will help to ensure that you do not lose material. It is also worth noting that the Amazon Digital Text Platform can respond in a confusing fashion if you exceed the maximum number of allowable characters in the "Description" field. The Platform may simply fail to accept your content, or alternately may truncate the content at about 850 characters. Make sure that you draft and save your Description content off-line so that it will be easy for you to edit and pare down the content if you run a little long. Once you have saved all of your entries on the Product Details screen you can proceed to the other two primary sections of the Digital Text Platform, where you will upload and preview your book or document, set its price, and publish it. You can change your product details any time by returning to the My Shelf tab on the Digital Text Platform "Dashboard". In order to change your product details later, just click the plus [+] sign next to "Enter Product Details" for a title, change your entries or add new information, and click "Save entries". If your item has already been published, click "Publish again" to update the details in the publication.

19. ***Upload and Preview Your Content***. Once your manuscript is has been subjected to careful proofreading, editing, and formatting, it is very easy to upload it. Under "Upload and Preview Book", just click on the "Browse" button and locate the file. Take the time to make sure you have located the correct draft or version of your content, and then click on "Upload," and the process begins. Most documents require just a few moments to upload, if you have a broadband Internet connection. Once the upload is complete, the Digital Text Platform will display a message informing you that your content has been successfully uploaded and converted. Once this message is displayed, it is well worth your time and effort to complete a thorough preview to look for formatting errors or editing deficiencies. You can go back to your document on your own computer, make necessary changes, and upload it again as many times as are necessary to get your document into perfect shape.

20. ***Set Your Price***. The final step before you click on the "Publish" button is to set a price for your content. Setting prices is always a complex process that must take into consideration issues such as value, competition, marketing and cost. Early indications are that Amazon is setting Kindle edition prices roughly equivalent to one-third to one-half of hardcover list princes, but this may change.

Check other content prices in the Kindle Store and set your price as you see fit, knowing that you will have no ongoing production costs for Kindle editions and that your "profit" or "author royalty" will amount to 35% of the Kindle price. You can always change your price later.

* * *

Once you have completed these 20 steps, both in preparation and "live" on Amazon's Digital Text Platform, you should be ready to publish your content successfully. All it takes now is a single click of the "Publish" button, and your content should be live in about 12 hours.

Good luck!

Of course, there are many other things you can do to help make each Kindle publication successful. In The Complete Step-by-Step Guide to Publishing Books, Articles & Other Content for the Amazon Kindle: Creating Your Own Success Story with New Technologies, I amplify these ideas in detail. I'll also help you understand how you can keep tabs on your progress.

* * *

Here's an additional tip:

Building Internal Hyperlinks into Your Table of Contents. As you may already be aware, traditional pagination is not very useful in Kindle books and documents and page references are consequently not very helpful in a Kindle book's Table of Contents. Kindle documents of all lengths employ bookmarks, "locations," and links as well as "Next Page" and "Back" features that are built into the Kindle's hardware. Page numbers would be problematic for several reasons, including the fact that the user-controlled text font size on the device has the effect of changing the number of "pages" in any document.

However, you can make your book's Kindle edition much more user-friendly by building hyperlinks into your Table of Contents. This is especially helpful for nonfiction books, but it can also make it easier for readers to go back, for instance, to find a favorite passage in a novel, a possible clue in a mystery, or any piece of text that they may not have thought to bookmark or annotate on their first reading.

The good news for authors and publishers is that it is very easy to add such links (or any other links) to your text. It may take you an extra 5 minutes or so when you are formatting your text for publication on Kindle's Digital Text Platform, a little longer if you have yet to create a Table of Contents. You don't need a lick of HTML knowledge to do it, because the commands for adding these links is built into Microsoft Word:

1. Create a Table of Contents for your document if you haven't done so already. The Table of Contents (and other front matter) should be part of the main document, located as it would be in a paper edition.

2. Make sure that each "chapter" in your Table of Contents corresponds to a "heading" in the document, formatted and set off with centering, extra lines of spacing and numerals to help Microsoft Word recognize it as a heading.

3. For each "chapter" in your Table of Contents, capture the chapter title (in the Table of Contents) with your mouse, right-click on the captured title, and choose "Hyperlink" in the little dialogue box that appears on your screen.

4. Choose "Place in this document" from the four options on the left of the "Insert Hyperlink" dialogue box that appears on your screen, and select "Headings" from the choices provided.

5. When you click on "Headings," Microsoft Word will show you a list of the headings that appear in your book or document. Click on the heading that matches the Table of Contents text that you have captured, and Word automatically creates the link.

Test your links before you upload your documents. An alternative approach to creating hyperlinks that allows greater fine-tuning and usually takes a little longer is available using the "Bookmarks" feature in the "Insert" pull-down menu in Microsoft Word. This feature is also appropriate for hyperlinking an index.

IX. Projecting a Kindle Future

How Many Kindles? Estimating the Current and Future "Installed Base" for the Kindle, And Why It Is Important

After a decade of interesting but ultimately failed efforts by various electronics manufacturers to hit the sweet spot of potential for an electronic book reader, Amazon launched the Kindle reader in November 2007. Although the Kindle quickly attracted critics and naysayers who predicted failure for the device, they failed to understand either Amazon's passionate commitment to the Kindle concept or how well the company is positioned to achieve dazzling success. Amazon's relationships with readers, early adopters, authors, and publishers provide the company with tremendous advantages over any competitor that might consider bringing an e-book reader to market, and Amazon has not squandered its opportunity. The device sold out about five hours after launch, sold over 200,000 units in its first six months (based on figures released by its Taiwan-based display-screen manufacturer), and is unlikely to look back after it reaches the one-million mark in Kindle units in circulation sometime early in 2009.

It is probably obvious to you already that I am keenly interested, as an author, in the commerce, technology, and business of publishing reading material of all kinds. Frankly, I have difficulty understanding how any writer – or any serious reader for that matter -- can fail to be interested in these matters, because they bear so heavily on the ways in which we can connect with readers and the economics of the writing life for all of us, from those who are doing fabulously well to those for whom the struggle to keep the wolf from the door is constant. In any case, if you are a Kindle owner or you are thinking about publishing your work for the Kindle, I strongly recommend that you find out as much as you can about what this device can mean for the future of reading and writing.

A good place to start is to navigate to the video of Charlie Rose interviewing Jeff Bezos on the Kindle's launch date (there's a link on A Kindle Home Page). It's worth spending the 54 minutes to listen, because it is worth knowing the extent of Bezos' commitment to this product from the first day of its launch, and to understand that his personal vision for the Kindle is explicitly inclusive of a fascinating range of possibilities for author and publisher experimentation. He speaks unabashedly about his belief that the Kindle eventually will allow readers to access every book ever written. It is equally clear that he expects, eventually, for a very large percentage of serious readers to own Kindles.

Of course, it would be easy to conclude that Bezos is just trying to line his pockets by playing cheerleader for the Kindle. Personally what I see is more significant than that. Here's a guy whose net worth is over $8 billion putting all of his credibility behind his claims and hopes for a revolutionary product, in an industry where his company is the single most influential player. Bezos' passion does not cinch the Kindle's success, but it persuades me to listen carefully to his efforts to express his vision for this product.

Some of the dialogue between Bezos and Rose seemed like the big tease:

Rose: "Why the name, 'Kindle?'"

Bezos: "To start a fire. "

R: "In your mind, your imagination, wherever?"

B: "Absolutely."

R: "To start a fire, to create a revolution in the world of books?"

B: "Absolutely."

What is remarkable, for now, is how little we know, numbers wise, about the Kindle. I had hoped that Amazon would share some information, when it released its quarterly 10-Q financial reports on January 30, 2008, concerning how many Kindles were sold and produced during the fourth quarter of 2007. Not a peep, outside of his statement that he was "super-excited" at demand for the Kindle. I have seen no disclosures and very little in the way of useful estimates on this question, which is important to me as a Kindle author. At best, when I wrote my first draft of this chapter in mid-February 2008, I was able to extrapolate a very conservative estimate of 20,000-plus "Kindles in circulation" based on the following:

* Of several titles I have offered for sale in Kindle editions, one title had sold 2,079 Kindle copies since it became available in late December, and it had averaged about 100 copies a day from January

23 to mid-February. This had been enough to place the title in the top 5 to 7 Kindle titles for a few weeks.

* It was my educated but unscientific guess that it was extremely unlikely that more than 1 out of 10 Kindle owners had downloaded this title, so I concluded crudely that there were at least 20,790 Kindles in circulation, and that Amazon had been shipping 500 to 1000 a day, on average. I believed at that point that these guesses were conservative, and that the real number was north of 40,000. But it was all just extrapolation and guesswork.

The April Amazon conference call came and went without any more guidance from the company about the number of Kindles in circulation, but at just about the same time, somebody finally sang. In an April 18 article on the Digitimes website, Rachel Kuo and Rodney Chan reported an announcement by the CEO of Taiwan-based Prime View International that it had been supplying Amazon and Sony with 60,000 to 80,000 e-reader display screens per month, and that about 60% of the total had been shipping to Amazon for the Kindle. Based on five months of history at the time, this suggested that there might be 180,000 to 240,000 Kindles in circulation as of May 1, a number higher than most estimates that had been made at that point.

Another way of looking at this metric is that of the 50 million monthly visitors to Amazon's website, less than half of 1% had purchased the single product most prominently displayed on that website for the previous six months. Seen that way, 180,000 Kindles after 6 months does not seem like so many.

Even more stunning was a forward-looking statement made by the CEO of publicly traded PVI in the same announcement that PVI's production of e-reader display screen would ramp up to 120,000 per month by the end of 2008. It does not matter if it occurs on Wall Street or in Tokyo or Taiwan -- if the CEO of a publicly traded company makes material pronouncements about the financial performance of that company, he better be telling the truth or he will face serious sanctions.

Assuming a very gradual ramp-up rate of 10,000 units per month, and allowing for gradual growth of Sony's production as part of the overall PVI order growth, any reasonable extrapolation from the PVI projections suggests that the number of Kindles in circulation would grow by 300 to 400 per cent from May 1 to the end of 2008, or perhaps allowing for a slower-than-likely manufacturing and fulfillment process, to the end of the first quarter of 2009. Without any regard for seasonality, I came up with this crude model for Kindle growth:

May 1, 2008 -- 180,000 to 240,000 Kindles in circulation

May: 48,000 new Kindles sold

June: 54,000 to 56,000 new Kindles sold

July: 60,000 to 64,000 new Kindles sold

August: 66,000 to 72,000 new Kindles sold

September: 72,000 to 80,000 new Kindles sold

October: 78,000 to 88,000 new Kindles sold

November: 84,000 to 96,000 new Kindles sold

December: 84,000 to 96,000 new Kindles sold

Total number of Kindles in circulation by late 2008 or early 2009: 726,000 to 838,000.

I made those projections about May 1, and although I can be a relentless tweaker where such things are concerned, most of what I have observed in the intermittent months supports them.

Despite the absence of information from Amazon, I have been reading speculation in the media and in the blogosphere on at least a weekly basis about how many Kindles are in circulation. Some estimates have seemed more plausible and calmly reasoned than others. Some, on the other hand, have based their extrapolations on laughable "indicators" such as the fact that they have yet to see any Kindles "in the wild" or the number of customer reviews posted on Amazon's Kindle product detail page. In a thoughtful and interesting recent post publishing exec and blogger Joe Wikert lamented the spate of polemical putdowns of the Kindle by obvious, fairly simplistic and uninteresting haters. It is no accident, of course. Since the late 1990s Amazon stock has been followed by a large and raucous element of stock-shorters, who do little to attract followers with the shrill and poorly reasoned content of their attacks. At the same time, Amazon's entry into the hardware manufacturing market has brought a lot of barking critics into the open, with a certain amount of lashing out by partisans of all things Apple. In January, Steve Jobs himself dismissed the Kindle rather baldly with the public statement that "the whole conception is flawed at the top because people don't read any more." Other i-ophiles seemed to see the Kindle as a threat because of journalists' frequent speculation that the Kindle might become for books what the iPod, the iPhone, and iTunes has been for music.

Although I find fascinating things to chew on in nearly every Joe Wikert blog post that I read, and I appreciate the fact that he referenced my Kindle user's guide very nicely and used it as the centerpiece of his estimate about the "installed base" of Kindles, I have to challenge his basic argument. Joe notes the number of copies of my piece that I have sold -- 21,112 as I write this, but who's counting? -- and makes an interesting extrapolation:

> With the benefit of zero insider information, I recently figured the Kindle installed base was between 5K and 10K, perhaps a bit more. But that was before I noticed Stephen Windwalker has sold about 20K copies of the preview to his Complete User's Guide to the Kindle. So while there are at least 20K Kindle owners out there, given the low price ($2.39) and popularity of Windwalker's preview, I tend to believe most Kindle owners bought it. If so, that probably means the installed base is in the 20K's and a far cry from iPod levels.

Here's my problem with Joe's math, or analysis, or both. Although I have been lucky to have my title in the #1 spot among Kindle Store bestsellers for a few weeks, it has been further down the list, in the range between #2 and #15, for over 80% of the time between February 1 and this writing. Various titles have placed ahead of my e-book in the Kindle Store sales rankings, including, for several weeks each, books such as Scott McClellan's White House tell-most, the latest Oprah selection, and every word that someone named Stephenie Meyer has ever written, among others. As I write this, my book is ranked #3 behind debut novelist David Wroblewski's 576-page literary thriller ***The Story of Edgar Sawtelle*** and an anti-Democrat screed by a scandal-plagued former Republican political consultant.

While I love thinking about the possibility that some day ***most*** Kindle owners might buy something that I write and published, the plain fact is that Kindle Store rankings, like main Amazon store sales rankings, are based upon number of units sold. All one has to do is look at the list of the top 25 sellers in the Kindle Store to conclude that, while most Kindle owners are reasonably affluent, they are otherwise a pretty diverse group. They do not skew significantly toward political conservatives, political liberals, Oprah followers, debut fiction readers, either gender, or any other demographic. So, what is the likely Kindle reader penetration rate of the aforementioned e-books? As much as I understand the appeal of bestsellers, I find it very hard to believe that more than 10% of Kindle owners have purchased and downloaded the David Sedaris book, the Wrobleski, the Dick Morris, or the Greg Mortensen. It just wouldn't make sense on its face, unless the readers were somehow able to download a crisp sawbuck along with their e-books.

But here's another way to look at it. Remember how long ***The Da Vinci Code*** sat atop the New York Times bestseller list? A year after its 2003 release by Doubleday, there were a little over 6 million copies in print, and I remember thinking to myself in the Spring of 2004 that it would have to fall from the bestseller list soon because, well, doesn't everyone who wants it have it by now? Wrong again, Gorilla Breath. During a three-year period it spent nearly 20 different periods, ranging in length from one week to 15 weeks, in the #1 bestseller spot. By 2006 it had spent nearly three years on the bestseller list and sold 60 million copies in 44 nations.

My point? It took a long time of continuously occupying the #1 position on the bestseller list for ***The Da Vinci Code*** to achieve its ultimate penetration of the total book market, and after a year it had achieved only 10% of that ultimate sales level. While I don't think that the universe of Kindle owners exactly mirrors the universe of all book buyers, there is little reason to think that it would be more monolithic in its selections. And none of the books that have outpaced my little e-book on the Kindle Store bestseller list has anything close to the commercial legs of Dan Brown's book.

So, back to where we started: what does all this tell us about how many Kindles are in circulation? If my title had continuously occupied the #1 position, it would be reasonable to think that it had been purchased by 10 to 12% of Kindle owners, and conceivably a higher percentage if there were any basis for thinking that there had been a big gap between the #1 position and the #2 position. But instead, the Kindle Store sales rankings have been relatively fluid within the top 25 spots, and since I have spent as much time between #5 and #10 as I have spent in the #1-#4 range, 10% penetration is the ceiling. The overall sales penetration of my title among Kindle owners is somewhere between 5 and 10%.

I've sold 21,000 copies of my book as of July 4, 2008. The installed base of Kindle owners is **somewhere between 210,000 and 420,000**. All of this is based on extrapolating from my sales figures and combining that information with an analysis of the Kindle Store bestseller list and book bestseller lists in general. I've been in the book business as an author, bookseller or publisher most of the time since 1986 and I do not mind asserting that I have been to night school with respect to what book bestseller lists can communicate.

But it is also worth noting that this analysis squares well with the earlier extrapolation based on the pronouncements of Amazon's Kindle display screen vendor. According to that extrapolation, as of July 1, there would be **somewhere between 282,000 and 344,000 Kindles in circulation**. Just so. While neither of these analyses can stand alone and be taken as gospel, they were arrived at independently and thus strengthen each other. But whether the current installed base is 20,000 or 300,000, I heartily agree with Joe Wikert's point that the Kindle is not likely to come anywhere near the iPod's installed base. Not, at least, in the next several years.

Why is it important? Obviously, if you are an Amazon shareholder, there could be thousands, or millions, of reasons why the success of the Kindle is important. But for Kindle owners, it is all about the natural symbiosis between platform success and product satisfaction. If the Kindle becomes a mainstream product rather than a novelty item, it should motivate both publishers and programmers to expand the selection of content and features available to Kindle owners.

Whatever the success of the Kindle in its early months, it is successful in spite of the fact that Amazon has yet to deliver much basis for confidence that it is making serious progress toward meeting Bezos' stated vision of Kindle access to "every book ever printed." Although there is surely some significant duplication of titles, the main Amazon store currently lists over 13 million titles for printed books. By comparison, the Kindle Store began last November with about 88,000 book titles and, in seven months since, has grown only to 137,000 books, 346 blogs, 20 newspapers, and 16 magazines. Although Amazon has done reasonably well with bestsellers, the slow pace of the Kindle's catalog growth is a disappointment to current Kindle owners and is bound to be a hindrance to Kindle unit sales.

What would it take for the Kindle to move into a much higher order of sales or rate of adoption?

A lot.

But we shouldn't forget Bezos' passion for the Kindle, Amazon's average monthly website traffic rate of over 50 million visitors, and the company's rather astonishing track record in emphasizing customer experience while transforming marketplace behavior. In the next chapter we'll take a look at some of the next-generation enhancements, combined with a possible sea change in mainstream reading behavior, which could boost the Kindle or a successor device into the 10-million owner range by the middle of the next decade. Fasten your safety belts.

X. The Golden Age of Kindle 2.0 and Beyond

Contents of This Chapter:

Find Some Pols to Push for a Green Tax Credit

Screen and Keyboard Freezes

Gifts

Make the Kindle More Kid-Friendly

Real USB Port or Bluetooth for Hardware Connectivity with Memory Devices, Keyboards, Sound Devices, etc.

Treat Kindle 1.0 Early Adopters with Some Respect

Not long ago (as I type away in July 2008) a reputable tech website posted some intriguing information stating that an unidentified "insider" had leaked information to the effect that two new versions of the Kindle would be released in late 2008 and early 2009. The second release, in 2009, would take advantage of continuing enhancements to the e-ink display technology and involve a larger (but not necessarily heavier) device with a larger, perhaps flexible screen. These display enhancements might include some of the technology advances involved in the forthcoming Readius device and the much-discussed October issue of Esquire magazine that will hit newsstands in September. I have no reason to doubt the story. It has been widely quoted and referenced as authoritative elsewhere on the web, despite some internal contradictions regarding timetable, its strangely worded notion that the new models would "hit stores," and its lack of attribution.

We've all got tons of great ideas about the improvements that we absolutely must have as Amazon releases the Kindle 2.0, 3.0 and beyond. Many of the ideas that have been suggested in various blogs and communities as well as in messages sent directly to Amazon at kindle-feedback@amazon.com, and I expect to see a good portion of them realized in future Kindle generations.

I've already participated in this process as an individual Kindle owner, and I will continue to do so. Here, rather than add my voice to those of thousands of other Kindle owners who have weighed in with good suggestions for fixes to the obvious design flaws such as those pesky next-page bars, I'm going to give short shrift (at the end of this chapter) to these obvious next-generation needs and instead take a different approach and try to suggest some enhancements of a more radical nature, changes that could create some serious viral energy to expand the reach and the function of the Kindle. Then I will suggest a roughly equal number of changes that would build upon the Kindle's concept and on Amazon's commitment to electronic reading generally by opening a big tent around the Kindle and its content and inviting programmers, publishers and, perhaps, even competitors inside.

You can blame me for these, but please, give me no credit for them. While it is true that some of these ideas occurred to me before I read about them somewhere else, others were generated by some of the truly creative and thoughtful people on other Kindle websites and communities, while readers of the beta versions of this book shared others with me via email. Many are mash-ups, if you will, of all three of these fountains of Kindle ideas, and this is as it should be. I will certainly try to give credit where I am aware that it should be given, but I am also bound to miss out here and there.

One last thing before we issue some suggestions. You should assume that everything that you read in this chapter is purely speculative, that neither I nor anyone referenced here has an authoritative inside source at Amazon, and that the fun little **Likelihood of Adoption** paragraphs and numerical values are simply one man's opinions.

Kindle Reading Subscriptions

Amazon launched the Kindle with a fairly rigid pricing scheme: customers would pay a relatively high price for the device, with two important promises as counterweights to that price:

they would be able to buy individual e-books at a significant discounted compared with the price for print-on-paper versions; and

they would receive other value for free or very close to free, including access through their Kindles to a wide and growing array of public domain content, to the Kindle's wireless web browser, and to other material that they could select, aggregate or send to their Kindles.

But this is not the only pricing model. Another perfectly reasonable approach -- one that is working well for Netflix and for Amazon subsidiary Audible.com -- would be for Amazon to allow

Kindle customers to purchase subscriptions to a certain amount of content each month, either in dollars or points or some other form of currency. Naturally, Amazon could provide a range of different price and service options, and would have to work out how this approach would affect its royalty payments to publishers. But the dollars that would be available to Amazon through a reliable monthly revenue stream of this nature would be more valuable than the dollars paid up front for the Kindle, so it is reasonable to expect that Amazon would consider reducing the up-front Kindle cost for customers who would commit to a subscription plan, just as Amazon and its partners offer discounts and rebates to their customers who commit to an extended cellular phone service plan. It might also be reasonable to expect that the subscription plan might be accompanied by discounts off the usual Kindle prices for electronic content.

Customer Experience: Buy your Kindle for $329 and sign up for the Kindle Readers' Plan for $29.95 a month to receive at least two full-length books plus one newspaper, one magazine, and one blog of your choice from the Kindle store.

Likelihood of Adoption (on a scale of 1 to 10): 7. One benefit of such a plan, for Kindle owners, is that it might help them budget their reading dollar. Is that a positive or a negative from Amazon's point of view?

Kindle Buffet

The idea of an all-you-can-eat Kindle Buffet is, of course, nothing more nor less than Kindle Reading Subscriptions on steroids. The basic notion is that a customer, in the course of buying his Kindle, could pay an annual or monthly fee for the right to download anything in the Kindle store anytime. Technology publisher O'Reilly Media has pioneered this approach successfully with its Safari Books Online service, which offers subscribers an impressive selection of books at a choice of two price points: an unlimited feast for $42.99 a month or a revolving 10-book bookshelf for $22.99.

Although the concept is appealing on its face, a real all-you-can-eat buffet involves considerable risk for Amazon and the potential for sticker shock for Kindle owners. Assuming no change in its payment arrangements with publishers, Amazon would probably have to require a monthly payment of $50 or more, or an annual payment of $500 or more, to support the gamble of the unlimited option. While some professional technology readers might spring for that kind of expense, it is not a mass consumer price-point.

The 10-book bookshelf makes much more sense, as it would reduce the chances of a buyer taking advantage of the system and saddling Amazon with publisher royalties for books he might never read. Still and all, one has to wonder what price point could make it all work for Amazon and for readers.

Customer Experience: Lay down $40 a month or $400 a year and never pay for an individual e-book again. It sounds great, but are your eyes bigger than your reading capacity, to mangle a phrase? The problem is that the price Amazon might have to charge to protect the buffet concept from abuse would probably be so high that only the most voracious readers could make it work for themselves financially. When Netflix sends me a DVD I know it is only going to take me two hours to watch it; books take me longer.

Likelihood of Adoption (on a scale of 1 to 10): 4. There's one way Amazon could make this one work, and of course it would have tremendous instant appeal. Offer the Kindle for $99 to customers who sign up for a two-year Kindle Buffet contract. If Amazon's master plan is to get as many Kindles out there as possible and then make money on their reading, this is the way to go. Of course, how could that not be the master plan for the company whose original mantra was "Get Big Fast?" Okay, it probably won't happen overnight, but let's change that 4 to a 7.

Kindle Groups

As many Kindle owners have already discovered, the device can be as convenient for reading professional memoranda, manuscripts and other privately sent documents as it is for reading the content one buys in the Kindle Store or the free books that originate from Project Gutenberg, feedbooks.com, or numerous other sites that offer free content. With KindleGroups, Amazon would offer any Kindle owner the opportunity, possibly for an annual fee, to establish a KindleGroups Transmitter account (I'm using this word because it communicates well for now, rather than because I like it) with up to 5 KindleGroups consisting of the johndoe@kindle.com email addresses of up to, say, 1,000 Kindle owners each (although it might well be in Amazon's interest to expand that number gratis). KindleGroups Transmitters, who would be the only ones paying the annual fee, could then send Kindle-compatible documents to all the members of their populated KindleGroups simply by sending such documents to the umbrella address of a particular target KindleGroup. Each recipient account could be charged the going micro-charge rate of 10 cents per conversion, unless Amazon decided the charge was counterproductive for KindleGroup members.

Companies, organizations, universities and other information-intensive groups would take advantage of this functionality by promoting the purchase of, or even bulk buying, Kindles for their members.

KindleGroups would help Amazon achieve an enormous increase in its penetration of corporate and other group-based markets. Naturally these Kindles would then lead to increased sales of Kindle editions, increased user time on the Amazon PC site, increased sales of all other Amazon products, and logarithmic increases in the spread of the kind of digital culture to which Amazon's future revenue is intrinsically tied.

These are the basics, I think. Since I ordinarily come at these things from a bookselling perspective, I've been thinking for a while that the time should come soon when Amazon should arrange with Stephen King or J.D. Salinger to release his or her next book for the Kindle 60 days ahead of print, and then keeping doing this about once a month. Of course Amazon already knows that: nothing sells TVs like must-see TV.

But then last week I was thinking about a community organizing outfit with which I worked back in my youth, ACORN. They've got a thousand or so staffers spread around the country, paying for data transmission, Blackberries, laptops, whatever. They probably have a dozen or more must-read internal memoranda each week, so I got to thinking about Kindlizing their staff communications, which in turn got me thinking that every other info-intensive corporation or association or agency in the country could profit from Kindle-connectedness.

I'm kind of jazzed about this idea. I'd love to hear what others think about it.

Customer Experience: People love staying connected with their Crackberries and iPhones, but these devices aren't primarily intended for reading and are not easy on the eyes once one moves beyond a two-sentence email or text message. The Kindle is ideal for reading longer memoranda, reports, and manuscripts, and once you (or your employer) springs for a Kindle you'll never have to read such documents on a tiny backlit screen again. Leave your laptop home, and your Kindle and smartphone will get you through most or all of what you'll need to do on most road trips. If you are a "transmitter," what's not to like about knowing that you can connect wirelessly with entire groups of staff, colleagues, or other group members, and share documents of any length, just by sending them to a single KindleGroups address. Even if Amazon imposed an annual cost of, say, $99 for transmitter accounts, remember that the Kindle's wireless connectivity is free and you'll see how nicely it compares with the steep monthly data costs for a Blackberry, iPhone, laptop, or other device.

Likelihood of Adoption (on a scale of 1 to 10): 7. I sent this idea to Jeff Bezos and his team a couple of months ago, but I didn't get any love. Maybe I am missing something -- there is a first time for everything -- but my take on this is that it would allow Amazon to start harvesting Kindle sales by the hundreds rather than individually. Of course there is absolutely no point in Amazon moving forward with the KindleGroups idea unless they also provide a "folders" or "Google labels" feature to make it easier to manage content on the Kindle Home and Content Manager screens.

Kindle Owners as Kindle Sellers

This elegant idea is the brainchild of Joe Wikert, blogger extraordinaire who has a day job as a publishing executive at John Wiley. Have I added my own two or three cents to it? Of course I have.

As with other early adopters, many Kindle owners tend to be somewhat evangelical buzz agents in spreading the word about the device and all it can do. I have to admit that when someone sees me out and about with my Kindle and asks about it, they better have 10 or 15 minutes to spare. Amazon has taken a couple of major steps in recognition of this propensity:

A prominently displayed "See a Kindle in Your City" page on the Amazon website, promoting the concept of meet-ups in cities and towns all over the country so that Kindle owners can show off their Kindles to prospective Kindle buyers. Although one might expect some reticence to participate in this day and age, early indications are that it is becoming a popular feature.

Right from the start, Amazon has offered a very attractive 10% Amazon Associates affiliate fee for all purchases from the Kindle store, including the Kindle itself. In other words, if you buy a Kindle through a link like this one embedded in my website, an email, or in any other content, Amazon will pay me 10% of your $359 purchase price. This can get lucrative in a hurry.

What happens when you combine these two initiatives? You get Joe Wikert's idea, and it is a keeper. Kindle owners are already carrying a lot of water for Amazon via word-of-mouth enthusiasm about how much they love their Kindles, and all Amazon would need to do to return a little love (and, in the end, greatly multiply the love they get back), would be, in Joe's words, to provide "something as bare-bones as one screen with a couple of text-entry boxes where we can put the prospective buyer's name and e-mail address .... thanks to the magic of Whispernet the info would go right to Amazon and they could then send the prospect a message with more info on the Kindle. They could also track you or I as the lead originator, so if an order results, we'd get credit for it."

Joe goes on to suggest some great operational ideas such as credit in the form of "a free Kindle book or two" and "a leader board showing the top 10 originators. There would be a lot of friendly competition to hit the #1 slot!" What's more viral than a proposal that could turn every Kindle into an order-taking device and every Kindle owner into a Kindle salesperson?

I love Joe's idea, and I believe it is well within the realm of Amazon's engineer capacities as well as its marketing vision. Although "a free Kindle book or two" would be nice, I tend to think the setting up each Kindle with an Amazon Associates tag would be more flexible for Kindle owners (who might want to use their credit to order groceries from Amazon) and also more powerful over the long haul for Amazon. Each Kindle owner could automatically receive an Amazon Associate tag and account (if he doesn't already have one), and the Kindle could be "wired" so that an email could go out automatically with a "click this link to order your Kindle now."

Amazon could even set it up so that the $35.90 affiliate fee could be split with the buyer, so that in addition to your handselling you would also be offering a prospective buyer a nice 5% discount for jumping on it right away through the link.

The profit motive would of course inspire a lot of evangelism - $17.95 a conversation is nothing to sneeze at. I feel a new chapter of my book percolating as I think about the possibilities here -- I hope you won't mind if I credit you for the idea when I wrote about it.

Customer Experience: Every time you someone asks you about your Kindle, you come a little closer to paying for it. 20 conversations and you are reading from a free Kindle! Duh?

Likelihood of Adoption (on a scale of 1 to 10): 9. What was it I said in the last paragraph. Yes, it was "Duh?" Not that there isn't a downside to all this viral thinking. Amazon would not want to be responsible for the marauding hordes of Kindle owners preying on potential buyers in every upscale community from La Jolla to Kennebunkport, or the guys sitting in those cushy easy chairs in every Starbucks with an "Ask me about my Kindle" sign taped to their foreheads.

Kindle Content Affiliate Program

If you liked the "Kindle Owners as Kindle Sellers" concept, you'll love the Kindle Content Affiliate Program. (I know, it needs a catchier name, which no doubt Amazon will develop. I'm just going for informative here, not sexy).

One of the features that I love in the Kindle Store is the ability to get a sample chapter of just about any Kindle edition sent wirelessly to my Kindle within a few seconds via the Whispernet. What I'm suggesting here is just a new Kindle-to-Kindle wrinkle that would allow Kindle owners to buzz to their Kindle-owning friends about the latest book their reading, with a brief note and a sample chapter. Once again, the engineering required would be a snap, and from any e-book you were reading you could click on the menu bar and pull up a screen that would allow you to type in a friend's kindle.com email address (or select it from a list of your Kindle contacts) and send off your note and sample with an easy-to-click invitation for your friend to buy the title that you recommend.

Since Amazon already established an affiliate account for you and your Kindle (see above), it would be easy for Amazon to pay you an affiliate fee whenever your recommendation results in a purchase by the friend you've contacted. Or, better yet, let Amazon split the affiliate fee so that 5% each goes to you and your friend.

Customer Experience: An idea like this one is bound to optimize the Kindle's astonishing potential for putting readers into contact with each other and with authors or publishers whom they wish to follow. The same things that customers enjoy about the recommendation features of the main Amazon site would be made even more seamless for Kindle owners. Meanwhile, it's yet another means for voracious readers to help defray their Kindle and Kindle Store expenses.

Likelihood of Adoption (on a scale of 1 to 10): 9. This one synchronizes chapter and verse with Amazon's signature marketing and customer experience strategies. It would also easy for Amazon to protect Kindle owners from spamming abuses of the feature by requiring that such messages originate from a Kindle and allowing Kindle owners to block particular senders.

Shop the Amazon Store Through a Kindle Gateway

Here's a conundrum for you. You know how easy it is to shop the Kindle Store from your Kindle? Pretty easy, right? (I suspect that most of us tend to do more of our Kindle shopping from our desktop or laptop computers, but that doesn't mean that a significant amount of folding money doesn't change hands in Kindle-based transactions).

So why doesn't Amazon make it just as easy for Kindle owners to use their Kindles to shop the main Kindle store? Kindle owners are probably more likely than just about any other group of customers that Amazon can identify to be Amazon loyalists, early adopters, significant spenders, and avid readers. That, my friends, is what we would call a demographic Grand Slam. It is so obviously in Amazon's interests to provide Kindle owners with a seamless Kindle-based gateway into all of the company's many main-store departments that I am surprised I haven't seen more discussion of this issue.

I got a chance to ask Jeff Bezos this question live on Tom Ashbrook's On Point program on NPR, and he said that the reason

Amazon had yet to open this gateway involved engineering obstacles. If they can't fix this one soon, it's time to hire some new engineers. This is money in the bank for Amazon.

Although Amazon has not wanted to release any information regarding Kindle sales, the company did offer a report, several months after the Kindle's launch, to the effect that Kindle owners were buying more print-on-paper books than they had purchased before they had their Kindles. This seemed strange, but if it is true, then it would probably also be true that they would be likely to buy more gourmet coffee, shoes, electronics, and office supplies from Amazon too -- especially if they could make some of those purchases directly on their Kindles.

Customer Experience: Frankly, this enhancement will probably be more of a win for Amazon than it will be for Kindle owners. For Amazon, it's cash. For Kindle owners, it's a minor convenience plus. But even though I don't expect the Kindle to make my coffee (for a couple more years, anyway), what's not to like about being able to order a case of gourmet coffee, a pair of shoes, or a new printer from my Kindle? For Kindle owners, we will know it is here when there's a new line on the menu screen off the Home screen, right under "Shop in Kindle Store," that reads "Shop in Amazon Store."

Likelihood of Adoption (on a scale of 1 to 10): 10. Hey, if Jeff said it is only engineering, then it is only a matter of time.

A Big Tent for Kindle Content Availability On Other Devices

One of the things that can make it fascinating to watch the way Amazon conducts business is that the company often confounds conventional expectations about its merchandising strategies. Just when it appears that Amazon is all about trying to sell one category of merchandise, they turn that appearance and its attendant assumptions on their heads with strategic moves aimed at maximizing sales in some other merchandise categories.

During the half decade following the company's rather humble origins in 1994, Amazon built a reputation as a bookseller with great prices, great service, and very good selection. Then, beginning gradually in 1999, Amazon opened its big selling tent to thousands of other online booksellers from individuals selling out of their homes or garages to major book retailers like Powell's and New York's famous Strand Bookstore as well as countless other entities between these two extremes of scale. While some analysts, competitors, and potential Amazon Marketplace sellers wondered aloud (or in print) why Amazon would want to invite competitors inside its tent where they could "cannibalize" Amazon's own sales even while they benefited from Amazon's valuable website real estate, the fundamental underlying truth was that Amazon was showing its allegiance to its primary business principle of making money by optimizing its customers' shopping experience in terms of selection, service, and price. Eventually it became clear to all concerned, as it was repeated again and again by Jeff Bezos and other Amazonians, that Amazon was just as happy to make money off a Marketplace seller's sales as to make money off sales from its own warehouses. (For a much more thorough exposition of these developments and how they have come to affect the world of bookselling, see "The Bookselling Business: How We Got Here," the second chapter of my full-length book ***Selling Used Books Online: The Complete Guide to Bookselling at Amazon's Marketplace and Other Online Sites***.)

I digress, but my point would be that, if we look at Amazon's history and its "customer experience" mission, it shouldn't surprise us to find that the company's ultimate purpose, with the Kindle, may not be to sell Kindles. By launching the Kindle and pushing hard in the general direction of making the Kindle format the industry standard, Amazon guarantees that:

* we are turning the corner toward a world in which e-books and various other electronic formats for the printed word will become more and more prevalent;

* rather than be a print-on-paper dinosaur condemned to losing its dead-tree customers gradually to e-books and web-based reading, Amazon will be a major player, and very likely the leading player, on these evolving electronic terrains of publishing and bookselling; and

* Amazon will have a primary seat at the table, and tremendous influence with publishers as well as readers, in determining how various e-book publishing standards such as epub, .mobi, and .azw are positioned and which, if any, gains dominance.

To consider how this evolution will be visible in the context of future generations of Kindles or their natural offspring, it may not be too simplistic or reductive to think about two questions:

first, when and whether Amazon will make it easy for Kindle owners to buy content for their Kindles from other sellers without having to jump through too many formatting and file-transferring hoops; and

second, when and whether Amazon will make it easy for the owners of other e-book devices to buy Kindle edition books from Amazon for use on their Readius, iPhone, Sony e-Reader or other gadgets.

The first possibility, of course, is more than a possibility. Right from the start, it has been possible for Kindle owners to download tens of thousands of titles from free and paid websites and to use Amazon's own file-formatting services to transfer them to their Kindles. I have no doubt that Amazon pays attention to the extent to which its customers use their Kindles for these purposes, both in absolute terms and as a ratio against the number of Kindle editions that customers purchase and download directly from the Kindle store. Providing these and other ancillary benefits for Kindle owners makes the Kindle more marketable, and reduces the likelihood that customers will start reading books on some other device, so of course it makes good sense for Amazon as a business proposition.

I further have no doubt that Amazon will remain alert to possibilities for ways to monetize its Kindle customers' access to content other than Kindle editions, and might well open a revenue-sharing gateway into its Kindle Store tent for electronic files from other sellers. Of course, if an electronic file created outside of Amazon's boundaries is sold to Kindle owners in Amazon's Kindle store, it may be a distinction without a difference to call that file something other than a Kindle edition.

(The central question that will dictate Amazon's approach to other sellers' content may revolve around how Amazon and book publishers deal with the .epub electronic publishing platform, which is some publishers' choice to become the standard. Understandably, publishers want to avoid a situation where Amazon holds monopoly power in the world of new, DRM-ed electronic content. It is important and worthwhile for alternatives such as .epub to be maintained so as to allow choice and, to be perfectly candid, to keep governments from coming after Amazon for monopolistic practices.)

Once we imagine these possibilities, it becomes quite easy to imagine a relatively seamless world in which the owners of other e-book readers can shop in the Kindle store. I found it fascinating that during a presentation at the Spring 2008 BEA trade show, without even being asked, Jeff Bezos volunteered the possibility that Amazon might make Kindle edition books available for download to other devices. After about a decade of Bezos-watching for fun and profit, I can tell you with confidence that, despite his raucous laugh and seeming spontaneity, the Amazon CEO does not blurt things out, especially at forums such as the BEA.

So, let's think about this. One of the Kindle's initial missions has been to be a game-changing device that will make e-book reading an attractive choice for large and growing numbers of readers. We are not there yet, but we are getting there, and it is clear already that the Kindle is changing the game in ways that none of its predecessors could achieve. The combination of the device's features, Amazon's reach both with readers and with publishers, and Amazon's relentless marketing commitment to the Kindle makes such change quite likely, if not inevitable.

Once the Kindle clears that hurdle, there will be more and more hardware competitors, but none of these hardware competitors is likely to possess Amazon's reach or marketing power. Some of these competing devices will be every bit as cool as the Kindle, if not cooler. Others will have their own loyalists simply because they offer the convergence features that are desired by specific customers.

Why wouldn't Amazon want to make its Kindle catalog available on these devices for the right price? If the company's strategy runs true to form, Amazon will continue to push the Kindle but will also, eventually, be perfectly happy to be the bookseller for other electronic reading devices whose manufacturers seek entry under the big tent of the Kindle catalog.

Pushing the Kindle, ultimately, will primarily be a way of pushing the content that is available in the Kindle Store. When it comes to figuring out the business strategies of cash- (or stock-) rich companies like Google and Amazon, it is always helpful to watch their acquisitions. Warren Buffet's Berkshire Hathaway may buy other companies because of their current and projected value, but Amazon buys other companies for market positioning in the process of implementing its business strategies. During the period leading up to its launch of the Kindle, Amazon made important purchases such as its acquisition Audible.com. At this writing (and this will change soon) the only electronic book catalog even close to Amazon's 163,000 is NetLibrary's 160,000. NetLibrary is an interesting entity -- it is owned by the nonprofit OCLC (Online Computer Library Center), but when NetLibrary was on the ascendant back in 2000 it was making important strategic purchases of its own, such as PeanutPress, which for a while was the leading purveyor of electronic content for the PalmPilot. If Amazon could find a way to acquire a company such as NetLibrary, I suspect it would do so, and I believe it would also tell a lot about Amazon's plans for crossing platforms and making an ever-growing catalog available to a growing range of devices.

Customer Experience: More content, and eventually, all content. What's not to like? In addition to making more money for Amazon, this approach would also make more money for the publishers and authors who publish for the Kindle using either the Kindle's .azw standard or the .mobi standard. Naturally, then, by making it easy for publishers and authors to access other electronic distribution channels simply by publishing for the Kindle, Amazon would be greatly enhancing the author and publisher benefit of Kindle publishing. This benefit, in turn, would help Amazon to come closer to its stated goal of making "every book ever published" available to Kindle readers, which would be pleasing to us as current Kindle owners and would also, in turn, help to expand the installed base of Kindles. What goes around comes around.

Likelihood of Adoption (on a scale of 1 to 10): 8. When Jeff speculates, I listen. Whether and when either of these developments occur, of course, will depend on Amazon's own notions about the effect of such changes on the Kindle brand, on Amazon's net income, and on the company's long-term vision of a world in which Amazon, through the Kindle and perhaps these other devices, is the company that provides readers with immediate electronic access to every book ever printed.

Shop and Play Amazon Music and Audio

The Kindle's audio features are just a taste of what they could become if Amazon takes some logical steps in building upon the features as they exist in version 1.0. With the original device you can transfer music, podcast, Audible.com and other audio files from your computer to your Kindle and listen to them directly on the Kindle.

While Audible.com files are organized and presented very nicely on the Kindle, the other kinds of audio files are presented poorly, so that you are left to listen to them in random order as if you were using an iPod shuffle. They also take up a great deal of the Kindle's limited storage capacity and it is not easy or straightforward to save them and access them on an SD card.

It makes sense for Amazon to make the Kindle a more manageable and user-friendly audio device, especially since Amazon is already positioning itself as a major player in providing audio content through its expanding selection of music and other downloads, its purchase of Audible.com, and the tremendous reach that the CreateSpace audio platform may soon provide for Amazon's catalog of indie and previously out-of-print music.

Here are the basics we ought to expect in Kindle audio functionality:

Direct purchase and download of Amazon music and other audio content from the Amazon or Kindle store via the Whispernet right to the Kindle;

Direct access to podcasts to be pushed to the Kindle from the Kindle or Amazon store or direct subscription;

User-friendly folder management for audio files on Kindle-compatible SD cards as well as on the Kindle's native storage.

Audible.com sampling on the Kindle, similar to the sampling features already available with Kindle text content.

Customer Experience: These enhancements should make the Kindle a more enjoyable multimedia device without getting in the way of the reading experience. The Kindle will never be an iPod, but with a little more work the audio functions can fit nicely with the device's primary functionality as a reader. Naturally, it will also be a nice feature for Kindle owners -- and a profitable one for Amazon -- if they can buy and download audio content directly to their Kindles.

Likelihood of Adoption (on a scale of 1 to 10): 9. It is likely that these enhancements can be achieved mainly through some tweaking of the Kindle software and Amazon website engineering. They will lead directly to increased sales and profitability for Amazon in its relatively new and interesting digitalized audio departments, and make the entire experience of Amazon a more seamless experience for Kindle owners. Translation of the previous two sentences: this one is a no-brainer.

Kindle Tribes

If all of this, including my writing of this book, were taking place 8 or 10 years ago, I would probably have called this concept "Kindle Reading Clubs," and made some reference to Oprah. But I won't do that. We're all very 2008 here, aren't we?

The noun "tribes" and the adjective "tribal" are the best words that I have seen to suit the ways in which different groups of us come together to influence each other and to filter and distinguish what is worthy or unworthy of attention and emulation in our cultures and subcultures. I could swear I coined the usage myself in chapters I was writing several years ago for what became my book Beyond the Literary-Industrial Complex, but it isn't important, and even if I thought of it myself it is not uncommon or iconic a usage that dozens or even hundreds of others could not also have hit upon it. I'm happy to share. It may even be derivative of some reading and writing that I did about ant colonies and Amazon buyers and sellers all the way back in 2002.

The Kindle has enormous potential as a cultural platform across which tribes of readers and writers can lead and follow one another to promote their tastes and standards and interests in literary and other forms of cultural expression. Of course, one can say, that is what already happens on the Internet and more specifically in thousands of specific Internet communities. The internet offers a viral post-advertising expansion of communication channels and platforms by which readers may communicate not only with each other but also inter-actively with writers, publishers, booksellers, and librarians about the content and quality of books and other media. Why do we need to add the Kindle and yet another layer of cultural tribalism?

Because it is such a natural opportunity, for starters. While I would not hazard much generalization or stereotyping about exactly what "kinds" of people comprise the roughly 300,000 Kindle owners as I write these words, it is reasonable to assume that they skew toward avid readers and early adopters. If there is also significant representation among people who speak up about what they like as readers by writing Amazon customer reviews, blog posts, and various kinds of commentary on social networking and other sites, all the better. The trick -- and it is a trick that I will leave largely to Amazon since Amazon's business model over the past 14 years has demonstrated incredible gifts and virtuosity in these areas -- is to figure out, and then to implement, the best ways for Kindle owners to engage in their own forms of tribal influence over what there is to read in the world, and what is actually worth reading.

While I am glad that the Kindle has a keyboard, I would not recommend the device for writing customer reviews, for instance. However, it would be easy for Amazon -- in the process of providing software updates -- to provide Kindle owners with the capacity to begin reaching out to one another and creating tribes and clans of affinity based on shared tastes in content, among other things. Amazon has already invested a great deal of effort in offering a fascinating array of features which are present on its website and highly pertinent to tribal organizing and sorting possibilities: offerings such as Amazon Friends, Amazon Communities, Interesting People, Amazon Purchase Circles, and Amazon Connect. It is my impression that most of these features are not yet heavily engaged by Amazon's huge customer base, but it is with some of these features that I would begin if I were one of Amazon's more creative types trying to begin to provide Kindle owners with the architecture for meaningful tribal behavior and organization around Kindle and other content. One can easily imagine the Kindle and its communities, with its huge (and mostly still untapped) potential for file-sharing, annotation, and networking, as a primary hub for such behavior if future price breaks and next-generation input enhancements allow.

Customer Experience: I've seriously copped out here, avoiding much real or concrete discussion of the actual feature set that it would take to empower Kindle-owning tribesmen and tribeswomen to take their natural viral behavior to new levels. My reticence comes less from any sense of a dearth of specific ideas here than from a realization that there could be dozens of great ideas in play. If Amazon's passionate commitment to the Kindle's potential is married to an equally intense passion, among large numbers of Kindle owners, to connect with other humans around comment, content, culture and community, the Kindle could yet be the most revolutionary technology device of the first part of this century.

Likelihood of Adoption (on a scale of 1 to 10): 9. We'll know it when we see it.

"Living Books" on the Kindle

I thought I had finished this chapter, and then I heard this fantastic, simple and elegant idea on Len Edgerly's excellent Kindle Chronicles podcast show. Imagine being able to read a book (or anything else) on the Kindle and share your highlights, annotations, and bookmarks with specifically chosen other Kindle owners -- business colleagues, family members, book club members selected by you in affinity groups that you can easily manage on your computer and choose on your computer. The concept, as Len noted in his low-key rollout of the idea during his August 1 podcast discussion with C.C. Chapman, would be similar to the document-sharing features available on Google Documents, which has become one of my favorites among Google's entire array of terrific Web-based services.

Book clubs and reading groups would never be the same. Reading would never be the same. More than any other single idea that I've hatched or seen, this one would deliver on the Kindle's potential to create a felicitous confluence of culture, community, content, comment, and commerce. You know, the 5 C's.

Am I jazzed about this one? More than words can say.

And, well, h'mm, I wonder what would be in it for Amazon.

Duh. This would be the Mother of all viral marketing concepts for selling both the Kindle as a device and Kindle editions of the content involved. Because, although you and I could select each other and all the other members of our Tuesday night book group to have access to each other's annotations, marginalia, highlights, and bookmarks, we would each, of course, have to buy our own copies of the Kindle edition books (or other content) involved.

Customer Experience: Bliss.

Likelihood of Adoption (on a scale of 1 to 10): 10. Right now I think Jeff Bezos is a visionary genius. If he doesn't do this I would think he was an idiot. But he will do it.

Other Fixes for Kindle 2.0 and Beyond

Let me be clear: the list that follows is every bit as important as the perhaps somewhat highfalutin ideas that I have shared above. But most of the ideas below should have been obvious to Amazon before the launch, and if they weren't, they have probably been suggested by dozens of Kindle owners since the launch. So I am really just adding my two cents worth here. If you would like to add your support for any of the ideas above or below, please make a point of sending an email to kindle-feedback@amazon.com with your ideas, your reasons, and your bona fides as a Kindle owner.

Folders and/or Labels. I'm going to be polite here and refrain from saying something like "what were they thinking not to have included this the first time," but one or both of these architectures for content organization within storage directories needs to available, and totally user-definable, on every Kindle. They should have the capacity to recognize the Kindle's native storage, computer storage, and supplemental storage in the form of SD cards, etc. I suppose that most Kindle owners will be more experienced in folder management, but after several years of using Gmail and other labels-based Google features I would love to have the label feature, which would allow me, for instance, to locate War and Peace both among "Great Russian Novels" and "Books I Have Yet to Finish," rather than having to pigeon-hole it in a single folder. Why not provide both folders and labels.

Size, Location, and Configuration of Bars, Buttons, and Switches. The size and scale of the "Next Page" and "Previous Page" bars is terrific when I am using my Kindle while wearing catcher's mitts on both hands. In other circumstances they are unnecessarily large and cause everyone who has ever used a Kindle to turn pages unintentionally. We all get better at this with the passage of time, experience, and the benefits of growing muscle memory, but it still happens at least once a day for me six months out, and that is too often. So, cut down on the size of the bars, and while you are at it, make it possible to use the on and off switches for the Kindle and its wireless feature without removing the Kindle from whatever cover one is using. And, with credit to C.C. Chapman at The Advance Guard, why not make it possible for Kindle owners to configure these bars, buttons and switches as they see fit?

The Kindle Display Screen. I love the Kindle display screen. I love the fact that it is not backlit, that it is easy on the eyes, that it is black and white with various shades of gray. But I know change is coming. I have read the articles from Tokyo and Taiwan about likely enhancements to the E Ink display technology, including much faster refresh, color, touch screen features, a flexible display medium that could be folded into the device like the screen in the prototype pictures of the Readius. All of this is very cool, and will be good for textbooks and other technical texts, for color-loving gadget heads, for better web browsing, and for my son Danny who reads Manga and does some pretty amazing graphics of his own. Truth is, these changes will probably also be good for me, but they may take some getting used to. So, I hope that some of these features (particularly the color screen and touch keyboard that should probably replace the thumb-twister that currently exists on the Kindle) will come with toggle switches so that early adopters like me can replicate the fond memories they have of their first Kindle reading experiences back in 2007-2008.

Writeable Screen. But if the Kindle is going to have a touch screen, why not go totally beyond the Kindle keyboard? Direct writing on the screen with a stylus would be the best option.

Adjustable Fonts. The six adjustable fonts are great for just about everyone. However, I have been told by a couple of extremely experienced human beings that they still have trouble reading even the largest size font of some documents. If possible, then it would be good if the Kindle with a couple of even larger options, as well as the capacity for readers to choose a clean "sans serif" font such as Arial Bold or Comic Sans, since such fonts can offset their lack of bookish visual appeal, for visually challenged readers at least, by offering a less cluttered and therefore more decipherable presentation.

Go Global. It is time for Amazon to begin the inevitable process of rolling out the Kindle beyond U.S. borders. (What am I saying? Of course Amazon has been working on this since before the November 2007 U.S. launch, but let's get it done.

I assume that each international launch will require its own wireless contract, and there may be issues concerning Amazon's potential control of the marketplace that get raised within the European Union, Canada or elsewhere. (Indeed such issues could well be the reason for the Kindle's failure to launch internationally so far, since in addition to being troubling and costly in their own right such issues could find ways to reverberate unpleasantly back to the U.S. both as legal matters and as negative brand issues).

Once these things are sorted out, it will be good for current Kindle owners for the Kindle to go global. Why? Well, for starters, there are 20 potential Kindle customers elsewhere in the world for every citizen of the U.S., and that market opportunity will be a boon for Amazon's efforts to expand the Kindle catalog of books, newspapers, magazines, blogs, and all manner of other content. Indeed, the potential for border-crossing culture and community, as the Kindle's terrain expands around the world, is truly exciting.

Open the Kindle Store to Accessories. Amazon should open the Kindle store to aftermarket products and accessories like Kindle covers, power and battery-related gadgets, SD cards, etc., so that Kindle owners can find them more easily both from their Kindles and their computers. Any concern that such a move might expose the Kindle to scamming hucksters should be cured easily by the customer review process that works so well for everything else in the Amazon store.

Find Some Pols to Push for a Green Tax Credit. Huh? Think Prius here. Indeed, if I were Jeff (wouldn't that be nice?) I'd insist that everyone associated with marketing the Kindle should go to school on Toyota's marketing history with the Prius. Prius sales and overall public awareness about the vehicle's fuel efficiency and earth-friendly branding were greatly enhanced by the availability of a sizeable tax credit for hybrid owners.

Why not the Kindle? While at first it may seem counter-intuitive to think of one's usage of an electronic device, replacing one's usage of something as organic as traditional books, as a way of reducing one's carbon footprint, the facts are clear that the Kindle is as green a product as any to be launched in this decade: paper and trees, shipping, ink, the Kindle's long-lasting and quickly rechargeable battery, warehousing with all its concomitant expenditures of energy and natural resources -- don't even get me started. I'm no scientist, but I've been impressed by more scientific minds than my own that have been brought to bear in making pronouncements such as the oft-repeated notion that, if everyone, in the U.S. were to switch to reading their newspapers electronically rather than on paper, the nation would automatically come into compliance with the Kyoto Protocols.

As with many other tax credits, the point of promoting legislation for a Kindle tax credit would be less about the dollars and more about the public awareness that it would foster. Amazon and its Amazillionaires have been sufficiently generous to politicians over the years that they shouldn't find it difficult to find a few who would be happy to carry the water in promoting a Kindle tax credit.

Screen and Keyboard Freezes. Maybe it is just my Kindle, but this happens way too often. If it is the price I am paying for having replaced the Kindle's native screensavers with pictures of my children, it is too high a price. This should be fixed! Now! (Or, well, if Amazon can't fix it, I need to come up with a way to offer 2-cent pushpins as "Kindle Resetting Devices" in the Kindle Store at a price point of $7.95 each).

Gifts. It's all well and good that it is possible to give gift certificates to Kindle owners for their future content purchases, but not good enough. Amazon needs to come up with a way for Amazon customers to gift specific Kindle edition content to Kindle owners. It's a no-brainer as a way for Kindlers to share books that they like with each other. When I gave my son a Kindle this Spring, it's natural that I would want to follow up with a book or two each month. Giving him a gift certificate's just not the same.

Make the Kindle More Kid-Friendly. We love to buy things for our kids. While I didn't let the Kindle's dearth of kid-friendly content keep me from buying a Kindle for my then 9-year-old son, it's sure to work that way for plenty of other folk. Making the Kindle kid-friendly will make kids want it, which is 99% equivalent in my family experience with kids getting it. Where to start? More children's books is the obvious place to begin, along with better audio features, easier music-transfer functionality and perhaps the introduction of a cool text recognition read-aloud feature. After that, color covers and a branded Hannah Montana edition of the Kindle should seal the deal.

Real USB Port or Bluetooth for Hardware Connectivity with Memory Devices, Keyboards, Sound Devices, etc. The Kindle is a Linux computer. It is important and understandable from a branding point of view that Amazon has marketed the device as a reading device, but the Kindle is a Linux computer. In time, it will be important to balance the need to keep it stripped down with the potential that can be unlocked by offering this minimal standard of hardware connectivity to go along its stunning wireless connectivity.

In the alternative, of course, Amazon could go the other way and skip hardware connectivity altogether and go straight to Bluetooth.

Treat Kindle 1.0 Early Adopters with Some Respect. Naturally, there will be some disappointment for Kindle 1.0 owners if they find they have missed out on lots o' fun with future generations of the Kindle. Those with deep pockets will doubtless buy each new model that comes along, but despite all the griping about the Kindle being so expensive, my extensive interactions with Kindle owners suggests to me that the Kindle market is not quite as upscale as some may think. Providing existing Kindle owners with a perk or two as these future-generation Kindles roll out would be a graceful way for Amazon to honor the importance of these customers' contribution to the Kindle's amazing success. How to do this? An electronic gift certificate for a couple of Kindle edition books? A below-market price offer on an upgrade to Kindle 2.0? A chance to resell their de-registered Kindle 1.0s on Amazon Marketplace? Let me count the ways.

c. Your Wish is Amazon's Command

Well, maybe not exactly.

But Amazon does want your feedback concerning the Kindle:

What works for you? What needs serious attention in Kindle 2.0?

What "experimental" features are definite "keepers"?

What is your wish list for enhancements to the next generation of the Kindle?

Frame your opinions and make democracy work in the land of the Kindle by emailing your feedback to kindle-feedback@amazon.com.

X. More Kindle Tips and Tricks

It's okay to try these at home. They have all been road-tested so that they will create no problems for your Kindle.

I. Play a Game on Your Kindle

From the "Home" screen, type "ALT+SHIFT+M" to activate a game of ***Minesweeper***. Click on "Menu" to change the "degree of difficulty" by altering dimensions and number of mines.

II. Keep a Photo Album on Your Kindle

This one is fun!

1. Connect your Kindle to your desktop and navigate through "My Computer" to your Kindle. It will probably be recognized as an "E" or "F" drive by your computer, depending on your hardware configuration. When you click on your Kindle to open it you will find that its memory is already configured with 3 folders called Audible, documents, and music.

2. Add a new folder called "**pictures**" alongside the 3 existing folders. (If you prefer, you can do the same thing on a SD extra-memory card.) Within the new "**pictures**" folder, create a subfolder for any group of pictures you want to be able to browse through. Name these subfolders so that you will recognize them when they show up on your Home" screen's list of titles. Then copy the applicable pictures -- they must be formatted as jpg, gif or png -- into each folder from your desktop computer. Disconnect your Kindle from your desktop after you have finished copying pictures, and your Kindle should return in a few seconds to your home page. **Important note: You must follow the exact instructions here and call the folder "pictures." If you call it "photos," for example, the Kindle will not recognize it.**

3. From "Home," type "ALT+Z" to prompt your Kindle to recognize the new subfolder as a "Book." Open the "Book" and use "Next Page" and "Previous Page" to browse through your Kindle photo album. Once you have opened the photo album, select "Menu" with your scroll wheel for additional options. Several commands on the local menu will at the bottom of the screen will allow you to adjust your view. You can also type "F" to set or leave "full screen mode."

4. Although it is essential that you name the primary photo album subdirectory "pictures," you can use other names within that subdirectory to organize your photo album.

III. Bookmark Any page

Bookmark any page you are on by pressing "ALT+B."

Note: These bookmarks will be saved and may make it possible to navigate more easily within your Kindle content. However, it is important to know that you do not need to use a bookmark to save the place where you left off reading. Any time that you leave a Kindle book or other document, the device will remember your place and return you there the next time you open that document.

IV. Page Navigation on Your Home Screen

While you are on your Kindle "Home" page, type any number and you will be taken immediately to the corresponding page of your "Home" listings. Provided, of course, that it exists. If you type 0 you will be taken to the first page, if you type a number greater than the number of your last page, you will be taken to the last page.

V. Alphabetic Navigation on Your Home Screen

While you are on a sorted (by title or author) Kindle "Home" page, type any letter d you will be taken immediately to the page on which the first entry beginning with that letter occurs. Provided, of course, that it exists.

VI. Move Quickly through a Long Document

Hold down the "ALT" key and depress "Next Page" or "Previous Page" to **move more quickly** through a document. This shortcut will navigate about 5% of the length of your document forward or backward.

VII. Check the Time

Get the **time**, in the time zone associated with your Kindle account, by pressing "ALT+T." The time will be expressed briefly at the bottom left of your screen: in digital mode ("4:24 PM") from the Home screen or in conversational mode ("Twenty-four past four") if you are reading.

VIII. Set Your Own Screen Saver

When viewing any picture in the Picture Viewer (see Keep a Photo Album on Your Kindle), type "ALT+SHIFT+0" to set that picture as your **screen saver**. But **PLEASE be careful** with this one; some graphics may freeze your screen or turn you to stone.

To remove custom screen savers from your Kindle, connect the Kindle to your computer via USB, go into the "System" folder and then into the "screen_saver" folder. Delete all files from that folder.

IX. Skip a Song

Tired of hearing one of your playlist songs a few too many times? Just type "ALT+F" while you are in Audio Play mode to proceed to the **next song** in shuffle sequence. Of course, you already know that you can get in and out of Audio Play mode by typing "ALT+P".

X. Justify Your Text, or Not

Set or get rid of "**Full Justification**" mode, from the font size screen, by typing simply "J" and selecting your choice.

XI. Slideshow

Enable a hands-free "**slideshow**" that will allow scanning, reading, or viewing of any document (including a photo album, of course), while you are in Kindle Reader mode, by typing "ALT-0." Then type "ALT-1" to start or "ALT-2" to stop the slideshow. I find this one is a great feature for reading while I am on an elliptical or treadmill. Calibrating my reading speed to the speed of the slideshow refresh can be a challenge, since I have not found a specific way to change the refresh speed, but visual capacity allowing, one can do something similar by adjusting the font size.

XII. Refresh Revised Content At No Charge

Here's ***a tip*** for Kindle readers and Kindle writers, if you haven't picked up on this already. One of the potentially cool and powerful features of the Kindle is that it allows anyone who has purchased a book or article on the Kindle to automatically receive the freshest version of that title, if it has been updated. All you have to do is go to Your Media Library in your Amazon account, click on the "Downloads" tab from the choices across the top, choose the title you want to refresh from those you have already purchased, and select the "Send wirelessly to your Kindle" button at the right. Presto, you have the new, improved version if there is one! The catch, of course, is that readers do not know when to seek out this refreshed content unless authors or publishers find a way to tell them. So, let me make a point here of asking: if you have purchased any titles from me and would like to get a heads up when an update is available, please shoot me an email at the email address below, tell me what title(s) you bought and anything else you want to tell me, and I will be sure to let you know if revisions are afoot!

XIII. Great Sources for Free Content for Your Kindle

Feedbooks -- at http://www.feedbooks.com -- features thousands of books in Kindle compatible MOBI format. Just create a free account, sign in, and download whatever you like. Once you download a title to your desktop it's easy to use your USB cable to copy it to your Kindle. If you don't have the cable handy, just email it to your Kindle email address and Amazon will send it to your Kindle. Don't be geek-phobic - these MOBI-formatted books look great on the Kindle, and there is even a Kindle help page for Feedbooks visitors at http://www.feedbooks.com/help/kindle. Feedbooks also provides tools for pushing free blog and periodical content to your Kindle and in general is a good service to keep up with.

Another great website for free books for your Kindle is ManyBooks. This site is wonderfully user-friendly -- just find a title by author, title, or the search field, select "Kindle" from the pull-down list of available formats, click on download, and the title will be on your computer drive within seconds so that you can shoot it on to your Kindle email address (or transfer it via USB) in another 15 seconds or so.

For a long list of other websites that feature free content that you may transfer to your Kindle, see A Kindle Home Page and scroll down to the "Free Books" listings.

XIV. Save and Print a Screenshot with Your Kindle

You can save a screenshot of whatever you are viewing on your Kindle screen (except the Kindle's screensavers). This feature requires that you have an active SD memory card installed in your Kindle. Just press Alt-Shift-G to make your screenshot and a gif file of the shot will be save in the root directory of your SD card. (Hold down the ALT and SHIFT keys simultaneously rather than consecutively, then press the "G.")

To access the file, connect your Kindle to your desktop or notebook computer via the Kindle's USB cable and check the SD card's root directory. (Note: your computer will show the SD card directory **alongside** your Kindle's directory, rather than **within** it). You will then be able to print a copy of the screen from your computer.

XV. The Joys of Quick, Early Delivery of Kindle Periodicals

Although some current and potential Kindle owners bristle at the idea of paying Amazon for newspaper, magazine, or blog content, I don't mind admitting that the Kindle hits the sweet spot when it comes to newspapers and magazines (except for the problem of such limited selection). I am charmed by the fact a very readable version of the New York Times arrives on my Kindle Home screen around 5 a.m. Eastern each day, and that the magazines to which I choose to subscribe often get to me before they reach mail-order subscribers or newsstand buyers. That's worth a lot in terms of convenience and real-time information, and it will be worth even more as the selection expands.

XVI. Optimizing the Powers of Kindle Search

Like Google Desktop and Google Search, the Kindle has the power to use a single search to probe through your onboard Kindle documents, your onboard dictionary, Wikipedia, the web, and the Amazon Kindle Store for all occurrences of any given word, term, or phrase that you provide. Just click on the "SEARCH" button on the keyboard's bottom row, type in your search words, and use the scroll wheel to click on "Go." To fine tune your search to so that it is applied to specific areas such as Wikipedia, the Amazon store, or the web only, use the commands listed here.

To limit your Kindle search to specific universes such as the Kindle Store, Wikipedia, or the web, type your search term into the search field with the following prefixes separated by a space:

@web: Web Browser
@wiki: Wikipedia
@store: Kindle Store
@time: Time
@help: List of supported "@" shortcuts

The Kindle search process is often a quicker and smoother way to reach specific web destinations, as compared to opening the web browser as a separate step from the Kindle home screen. If your wireless switch is in the "off" position, of course, your search will be limited to documents that you have downloaded or emailed to your Kindle, and to your onboard dictionary. You can also begin a dictionary search by scrolling up and clicking next to any line in a document, and selecting "Lookup" from the onscreen menu.

One other lesser-known use of the Kindle's search powers is that they allow you to find books and other content without knowing their titles. Just type in "Let us go then you and I" in the search input field of my Kindle and it will come up with the title Prufrock and Other Observations, by T.S. Eliot, which I previously purchased and downloaded to my Kindle, as well as references in Wikipedia and elsewhere on the web.

However, it is worth mentioning that this feature also exposes two flaws of Kindle version 1.0. First, the entire Kindle edition catalog ought to be automatically searchable from anyone's Kindle, within the same constraints that apply to Amazon's "Search Inside the Book" program -- it would promote sales, of course, and it would also mirror the customer experience in the main store. But alas, no such luck. Second, and this one is a shocker, the Amazon main store is not searchable or even easily accessible from the Kindle! What are they thinking?

XVII. Using Your Kindle as an Audio Device

The Kindle comes with a built-in MP3 player and works seamlessly as a listening device for Audible.com listening files. The built-in speakers may not impress you, but use the audio-jack to the left of the USB slot at the bottom of the Kindle to connect it to a speaker or headset and the sound quality isn't bad. Further to the right of the Kindle's bottom edge, you will find "down" and "up" volume-control buttons.

Just tap Alt-P to begin or end use of the Kindle's audio feature, and use Alt-F anytime to skip to the next track. You'll generally be operating blind, since the Kindle plays whatever in its listening queue in random "shuffle" order without any on-screen reference. In order to get listening material on your Kindle you must transfer it from your computer, using the Kindle's USB cable, into your Kindle's native "music" file.

I find the best way to manage the music I want to hear on my Kindle is to create several "playlist" folders in the top-level Kindle directory, each representing an appropriate selection for a particular situation. I might listen to jazz while reading a book, or something a bit more lyric-intensive while reading the New York Times. By moving a certain playlist into the Kindle's "music" folder -- the only folder from which the Kindle will recognize and play music -- I can suit my listening to my situation in a couple of key strokes while the Kindle is connected to my computer.

It is also a simple matter, following these same steps, to listen to podcasts on my Kindle once I move them from my computer to the Kindle's "music" folder.

XVIII. Listening to Audible.com Content on Kindle

In addition to the music and podcasts to which you can listen on your Kindle after you store them in your Kindle's "music" folder via USB connection with your Kindle, you can also purchase and download or transfer Audible.com content and listen to it on your Kindle. Fortunately, Audible.com files come with better navigational enhancements than other audio files for Kindle listening, and when you enter Audible.com for the first time as a Kindle user (http://www.audible.com/kindle) you will be invited to get a free Audible.com book as a Gold plan customer with a free month of Audible.com service.

Unlike Kindle edition books that can purchased and downloaded directly from, and with, your Kindle, you'll need to use your computer to purchase and download content from Audible.com. (Since Amazon purchased Audible.com around the time of the Kindle launch, it is fair to expect that Audible.com connectivity for Kindle users may well be enhanced at some point in the future).

For now, purchase your content and use the free Audible Manager software on the site to download it to your computer, then transfer the content to your Kindle's native "audible" folder using your USB connection. If you are using a Mac, you may not be able to download Audible.com content unless you are using Windows-emulation software. When prompted by Audible Manager to select your listening device's "Audio Format Sound Quality," you can choose 2, 3 or 4 for Kindle compatibility. The best quality, and the largest file size, comes with selection 4 -- whether you choose this option may depend on your download speed and on the file space you have available on your Kindle and any SD memory cards.

Navigate to http://www.audible.com/kindle and sign up if you have not done so already. Download the Audible Manager software to your computer and re-start your web browser. Connect your Kindle to your computer via USB and "activate" the Kindle as your listening device within Audible Manager. Once you have purchased listening content, you will be able to copy it to your Kindle and listen to it there.

Once you have transferred Audible content to your Kindle you should be able to access it directly from your Home screen with your scroll wheel, just as you would a Kindle book or other content. Look for a tiny speaker icon next to the Audible.com content.

Once you've opened anAudible.com file, just use the onscreen navigation menu to move among your options including Beginning, Previous Section, Next Section, Back 30 seconds, Forward 30 seconds, and a Play/Pause toggle.

You'll have several listening options, including the rather tinny built-in speakers. For a better experience, use the audio-jack to the left of the USB slot at the bottom of the Kindle to connect it to a speaker or headset and the sound quality isn't bad. That jack will also work if you have an automobile with an MP3 jack. Further to the right of the Kindle's bottom edge, you will find "down" and "up" volume-control buttons. (Tip: If you don't do a lot of Kindle listening and your first Audible file doesn't seem to be starting for you, make sure that the volume is turned up.)

XIX. Returning a Kindle Store Purchase

According to Kindle's customer service team, you can return any item purchased from the Kindle Store within seven days of purchase. This, of course, is the kind of "tip" that any author or publisher provides with some trepidation.

To make sure you get prompt, helpful customer service, gather the order ID number of the Kindle purchase that you wish to return, sign into your Amazon account, and contact Kindle Customer Service via email. Navigate to http://www.amazon.com/kindlesupport and click on the orange "Contact Us" button at the right of the screen. If you prefer to use the telephone, call Kindle Customer Service at 1-866-321-8851 or 206-266-0927.

Just tell Customer Service what you would like to return and why, and you should promptly receive an email message something like this in your Inbox:

"I've requested a refund for the purchase and removed the item from Your Media Library. If the item is still on your Kindle, please delete that copy. After the refund is issued, you will no longer be able to access it. I've included instructions for removing an item from your Kindle below. Refunds are issued to the payment method used to make the original purchase and usually complete within 2 to 3 business days."

XX. An Inexpensive Daily Planner Utility for Kindle

This won't appeal to everyone, but for less than two dollars, author Stephen M. Hou has provided a handy Kindle calendar with which you can use the Kindle's annotation, bookmarking, and highlighting features to turn it into a rudimentary daily planner. If you already use a Blackberry or other PDA device, you won't be interested in this. But if you are one of the thousands of Kindle owners who is trying to get the most out of your Kindle so that it is the only device you carry with you, this product may be worth its price. Here's the link: http://www.amazon.com/2008-Daily-Planner-Amazon-Kindle/dp/B001997BJO/ebest

If you like the idea but would prefer a simple monthly calendar, Hou also has a product for you:

http://www.amazon.com/2008-Monthly-Calendar-Amazon-Kindle/dp/B0019DRVFE/ebest

And for those with special long-term calendar needs, he has produced a two-hundred-year (1901-2100) calendar:

http://www.amazon.com/1901-2100-Monthly-Calendar-Amazon-Kindle/dp/B001BDD430

XXI. Using Gift Cards, Gift Certificates, & Promotional Certificates to Give or Purchase Kindle Content

Although, unfortunately, it is currently impossible to give Kindle content directly as a gift to another Kindle owner, thc closest work-around involves using gift cards or gift certificates. Here's the drill straight from Kindle Support on how to use these forms of Amazon currency with a Kindle:

> *If you've redeemed an Amazon Gift Card, Gift Certificate, or Promotional Certificate to your Amazon.com account, any available balance will be used for your Kindle store purchase before your credit or debit card is charged. Your Amazon.com account must list a valid 1-Click payment method even if you intend to pay for your purchase with a Gift Card balance. Your Gift Card balance cannot be used to pay for subscription content from the Kindle store.*
>
> *To redeem a Gift Card to Your Account:*
>
> *1. Visit www.amazon.com/youraccount.*
>
> *2. Click "Apply a gift card to your account."*
>
> *3. Sign in with your e-mail address and password.*
>
> *4. Enter your claim code and click "Redeem now." Your funds will automatically be applied to your next order.*

To purchase an Amazon gift certificate or gift card for someone (including yourself), just visit this page at Amazon.

XXII. Recover Deleted Content At No Charge

It's not the end of the world if you delete a book that you have previously purchased from your Kindle and decide later that you want it back. Whether you erased the content from your Kindle accidentally or because you need to clear some space in your Kindle's storage capacity, all you have to do is go to Your Media Library in your Amazon account, click on the "Downloads" tab from the choices across the top, and select kindle books from the pulldown menu there. Choose the title you want to refresh from those you have already purchased, and select the "Send wirelessly to your Kindle" button at the right. Presto, your content will be restored to your Kindle without any additional charge.

You can also accomplish the same thing with a USB transfer by selecting that option rather than the wireless transfer, and following the USB transfer instructions in Downloading Kindle Editions Via USB Cable in Chapter VII - Traveling with Your Kindle.

Appendices

Kindle Links

Please feel free to share this list of links with others or paste it (or elements of it) into your blog or website. This material is also available online on a single web page at A Kindle Home Page.

Kindle owners, although these links can be used directly from your Kindle's experimental web browser, generally I don't recommend that approach, except in a pinch, because it will tend to slow down (and sometimes freeze up!) your Kindle. With a few exceptions (like the Gmail and other stripped down Google Mobile pages that work nicely on a Kindle), you'll do better to use these links either from a Word document or from A Kindle Home Page. If you'd like to receive these links as a Word document, just send an email to indieKindle@gmail.com with "Please Send Links" in the subject line.

I Kindle Shortcuts and Support

II Guides and Manuals for Kindle Users

III Kindle Blogs and Communities

IV Kindle Bestseller Lists

V Getting Free Content for Your Kindle

VI Publishing Content for the Kindle

VII Kindle Accessories

I - Kindle Shortcuts and Support

Google Mobile products page, featuring Gmail, Search, Maps, Calendar, Google Documents, a "411" telephone lookup service, SMS/texting, News, Photos, Reader, Blogger, and Notebook

Your Media Library Page on Amazon

Amazon Gift Card (currently, the only way to give Kindle books to another Kindle owner as gifts)

Mobipocket Reader 6.1

II - Documentation and Manuals for Kindle Users

The Complete User's Guide to the Amazing Amazon Kindle (Kindle Edition)

Graphics for the Kindle by Manuel Burgos

Kindle User Guide and Amazon Kindle Support (Amazon Publication)

Amazon Kindle Terms & Conditions: License Agreement and Terms of Use

Kindle Fan Guide (Kindle Store Version) (Free PDF Version)

III - Kindle Blogs, Podcasts and Communities

A Kindle Home Page

The Kindle Chronicles

indieKindle: a web resource for readers, authors, and indie publishers oriented generally but not exclusively around the amazing Amazon Kindle

Kindle Korner

Joe Wikert's Kindleville Blog

Windwalker's AmazonConnect Author Blog

eBook Reporter

Mike Elgan's Book of Kindle blog

The Kindle Reader

Kindleholic and Loving It.....

Technorati Listings of Kindle Blogs

Amazon Kindle's In-House Blog

IV -- Kindle and Amazon Bestseller Lists

For those who know something about me and consequently know that I am an ardent devotee of The Long Tail, you may wonder why I am trafficking in bestseller lists here.

Simple reason.

Amazon bestseller lists are the greatest gateway I have ever found to interesting "long tail" discoveries -- begin with any such list and keep searching and you will get into more and more interesting terrain as your search becomes finer and finer. And along the way you'll get plenty of help from "the wisdom of crowds."

Kindle Store Bestsellers

Kindle Store Bestsellers: Books Only

Kindle Store Bestsellers: Newspapers Only

Kindle Store Bestsellers: Blogs Only

Kindle Store Bestsellers: Magazines & Journals Only

Kindle Store Bestsellers: Fiction

Kindle Store Bestsellers: Nonfiction

Kindle Store Bestsellers: Hot New Releases (This includes titles released within the past 90 days).

Kindle Store Bestsellers: Movers & Shakers (This highly volatile hour-by-hour list shows the titles from the top 400 Kindle store bestsellers that have experienced the greatest percentage jump in sales rankings during the past 24 hours. For instance, a title that has jumped from #7 to #2 will show a 250% climb).

Kindle Store Bestsellers: Publishing & Books

Kindle Store Bestsellers: Literary Fiction

Kindle Store Bestsellers: Contemporary Fiction

Kindle Store Bestsellers: Science Fiction

Kindle Store Bestsellers: Fantasy

Kindle Store Bestsellers: Romance

Kindle Store Bestsellers: Gay & Lesbian Fiction

Kindle Store Bestsellers: Mystery & Thrillers

Kindle Store Bestsellers: Children's Books

Kindle Store Bestsellers: Children's Fiction

Kindle Store Bestsellers: Advice & How-To

Kindle Store Bestsellers: Self-Help

Kindle Store Bestsellers: Personal Transformation

Kindle Store Bestsellers: Health, Mind & Body

Kindle Store Bestsellers: Business & Investing

Kindle Store Bestsellers: Marketing & Sales

Kindle Store Bestsellers: Personal Finance

Kindle Store Bestsellers: Small Business & Entrepreneurship

Kindle Store Bestsellers: Investing

Kindle Store Bestsellers: Arts & Entertainment

Kindle Store Bestsellers: Biographies & Memoirs

Kindle Store Bestsellers: Computers & Internet

Kindle Store Bestsellers: History

Kindle Store Bestsellers: Humor

Kindle Store Bestsellers: Lifestyle & Home

Kindle Store Bestsellers: Parenting & Families

Kindle Store Bestsellers: Gay & Lesbian

Kindle Store Bestsellers: Politics & Current Events

Kindle Store Bestsellers: Reference

Kindle Store Bestsellers: Religion & Spirituality

Kindle Store Bestsellers: Science

Kindle Store Bestsellers: Sports

Kindle Store Bestsellers: Travel

Other Amazon Category Lists of Special Interest To Kindle Owners

Bestsellers in Books

Bestsellers in Magazines

Bestsellers in Amazon Unbox Digital Video Movies

Bestsellers in MP3s and Digital Music (Kindle Compatible)

Bestsellers in Music on Disc

Bestsellers in Computers and Computer Hardware

Bestsellers in Office Products

Bestsellers in Software

Bestsellers in Cell Phones and Wireless Service

Bestsellers in Camera, Video, and Photo

Bestsellers in Electronics

Bestsellers in Grocery

Bestsellers in Gourmet Foods

Bestsellers in Home and Personal Care

Bestsellers in Home and Garden

Bestsellers in Jewelry

Bestsellers in Movies and TV on DVD

Bestsellers in Musical Instruments and Musicians' Gear

Bestsellers in Sporting Goods

Bestsellers in Video Games and Consoles

Bestsellers in Toys and Games

V - Getting Free Content for Your Kindle

Baen Free Library

Creative Commons

Digital Book Index

Dartmouth College: E-Books in the Public Domain

Feedbooks.com

Kindle Download Guide from Feedbooks.com

Fictionwise Free Books

Free TechBooks.com

Google Book Search

Internet Archive

Librivox

ManyBooks.net

Mobipocket Free E-Books

Munseys

Online Books Page

Podiobooks

Project Gutenberg

Scribd

Technical Books Online

Wikibooks

World Public Library

Wowio

VII -- The Kindle and Kindle Accessories

Kindle: Amazon's New Wireless Reading Device

Amazon Gift Card (the only way to give Kindle books to another Kindle owner)

Executive Case for Amazon Kindle, Black by M-edge

Mighty Bright XtraFlex2 Light - Black

Amazon Kindle Book Cover

Amazon Kindle Battery

Amazon Kindle USB Cable

Amazon Kindle Power Adapter

iGo A00 Power Tip for Amazon Kindle

Kingston 2GB Secure Digital Memory Card

Kindle Reader Messenger Bag

The Transcend 8GB HC SecureDigital (SDHC) Memory Card with USB 2.0 Card Reader + Universal Memory Card Case + 5-Piece Cleaning Kit is available from Amazon 3rd party sellers at a price of $39.95 plus $9.95 S&H

Bibliography

Books and Manuals

Amazon.com, "About Your Kindle"

Amazon.com, Kindle User's Guide.

Stephen Windwalker, Beyond the Literary-Industrial Complex: Using New Technologies to Unleash an Indie Publishing Movement. Harvard Perspectives Press. 200 pages, May 2008.

Download for Kindle

Purchase from Amazon (Paperback)

Manuel Burgos, Graphics on the Kindle. Rare Arts Communications. April 24, 2008

Download for Kindle

Blogs, Podcasts and Websites

The Kindle Chronicles

Kindleville

A Kindle Home Page

Stephen Windwalker's AmazonConnect Blog

Harvard Perspectives Press Website

Frequently Asked Questions About the Amazon Kindle

About This Book

Q. How should I use this book?

A. See Chapter 1 - How to Use this Book

Q. How can I get a link-enabled copy of this book emailed to me so that I can access the links from my computer?

A. See the section entitled Get Your Own Link-Enabled Copy of This Book On Your Computer under An Invitation to Readers.

Q. How do I purchase a paperback copy of this book?

A. The paperback will be released in September 2008 and will be available in the Amazon store with this link.

Q. How do I purchase a Kindle edition of this book?

A. From your computer, go to this detail page in the Kindle store. From your Kindle, go to the Kindle store and use the scroll-wheel to go to the "Search Store" field at the bottom of the Kindle display screen. Type in "Windwalker" and this book should appear at or near the top of the list of titles by this author.

Q. Can I purchase this book in electronic formats other than for the Kindle?

A. Yes, this book is available in the Mobipocket store for a wide range of electronic formats including the iPhone, the Blackberry, the Palm, your home computer, and other devices.

Scoping Out the Kindle

Q. What is a Kindle?

A. The Kindle is an electronic reading device manufactured by Amazon and launched in November 2007 at an initial retail price of $399, reduced a few months later to $359. It comes with a one-year warranty and is a decidedly unimposing, not very elegant gadget in an off-white plastic case with a QWERTY keyboard so tiny that you may not notice that it's there until you accidentally hit a key that causes the Kindle to navigate somewhere. The device is configured to work with a proprietary format (.azw) created by Amazon in order to allow Amazon to control Digital Rights Management (DRM) to protect itself and the authors and publishers who make content available through the Kindle store, but Amazon will also convert other files including personal documents that you send to your Kindle email address in text, Word, html, .prd, .mobi, or image format. For more information, see Chapter II -- What is a Kindle?

Q. How can I see a Kindle "in the wild" before buying one?

A. This may seem like a challenge, since Amazon doesn't have any physical stores and Amazon is the only authorized seller of the Kindle, but Amazon has rolled out a great potential fix for this problem. The Kindle Store now features a "See a Kindle in Your City" section with links to Kindles in a long and growing list of cities and towns to help you connect with Kindle owners so that you can see the device in person.

Q. Can I read Amazon's product documentation before I commit myself to buying a Kindle?

A. These documents are available on Amazon's website. There is a brief "About Your Kindle" start-up guide that comes in the box with the Kindle, a basic Kindle User's Guide that you will find on your Kindle when you turn it on (but you can also download it as a .pdf file from Amazon's website), and a License Agreement with terms and conditions that is also provided as an in-the-box hard copy and can also be viewed on Amazon's website.

Q. What's inside the Kindle?

A. See the section called What's Inside the Kindle? in Chapter II -- What is a Kindle?.

Q. What is e Ink?

A. E Ink is the electronic display technology utilized by the Kindle as well as the Sony e-Reader and several other current and forthcoming devices. It was developed by the E Ink Corporation, headquartered across the street from my son's school in Cambridge, Massachusetts and founded in 1997 by Joseph Jacobson, a professor in the MIT Media Lab. After E Ink partnered with another company in 1999 to develop and market the technology, the business and its related patents was sold to Taiwan-based Prime View International (PVI) in 2001. PVI is now the leading manufacturer of electronic reader displays in the world, with about 90% of the market.

Up until mid-2008 e Ink displays have been manufactured in primarily in hard-surface and black-and-white, but prototypes displayed at industry shows during 2008 suggest that color and folding or flexible-surface, plastic film displays may be available in a matter of months. Naturally, there has been considerable discussion of the possibility that such enhancements may be rolled out by Amazon in a next-generation Kindle as early as late 2008 or early 2009.

The basic elements of the e-Ink technology involves millions of tiny black and white microcapsules which re-organize themselves into a new image each time a negative electronic field is applied, e.g., with each turn of a Kindle edition's page.

Q. What is the Kindle's wireless "Whispernet" service?

A. See Chapter IV - <u>The Amazon Kindle Basic Web Wireless Service: Why It Is a Revolutionary Feature, and Why Amazon Should Keep It Free or Cheap</u>.

Q. How often will I need to recharge the Kindle's battery?

A. It depends on how you use it. Generally it should give you back something close to Amazon's claims of one-day battery life when the wireless switch is "on" and up to one week of battery life when the wireless switch is "off." Keep the wireless switch "off" except when you are using the wireless, and the battery will last a lot longer. Using the Kindle's audio features will also consume more battery power than reading.

Q. How long does it take to recharge the battery?

A. It shouldn't take more than 2 hours, and generally you will find that if you plug it in for 30 to 60 minutes each day (or night) your battery will remain pretty strong. You can use the Kindle, by the way, while it is recharging.

Q. How will I know when the battery is fully charged?

A. When the battery is being charged, you will see an amber light next to the power adapter jack. When the amber light goes off, it means either that the battery is fully charged or that the power adapter is not plugged in at one end or the other. Once you disconnect the power adapter, you will see a graphic at the bottom of the Kindle screen that registers the extent to which the battery is charged.

Buying a Kindle

Q. How do I purchase an Amazon Kindle?

A. Here's a direct link to the Kindle's detail page at Amazon.com, where you can purchase a Kindle for $359 with free two-day shipping.

Q. What accessories do I need to order when I purchase a Kindle?

A. None. Everything that you need -- except the reading content -- comes in the box with the Kindle, including the battery, the cover, the USB cable, and the AC power adapter cord to recharge the battery. That being said, it might not be a bad idea to order the Kindle edition of this book. And of course, you may be interested in styling and tricking out your Kindle with some of the accessories that you can find in the Kindle store. If you plan to travel with your Kindle, you may also find it a good investment to pay $20 for an alternate battery. Gomadic also sells a convenient "Emergency AA Battery Charge Extender" for the Kindle right on the Amazon site. Another vendor, iGo Everywhere, offers several different Kindle chargers and a kit that includes both a wall (AC) and auto (DC) charger as well as retractable cable.

One other essential Kindle accessory -- that you will probably be able to find in your own household or office -- is a device to use in the Kindle's reset pinhole under the back cover. Some use a paper clip. I find a red pushpin to be more elegant, even if it begins to make the area at the bottom inside base of the Kindle's cover begin to look like a junkie's arm.

Q. Can I begin ordering content for my Kindle before I buy the Kindle?

A. No. Once you have placed your order for a Kindle, however, it will be registered to your account so that you may begin ordering Kindle editions of books and subscriptions to Kindle periodicals and blogs.

Q. How do I buy and install an SD memory card to expand my Kindle's memory?

A. See Adding an SD Card to Your Kindle in Chapter III -- Kindle Basics.

Reading on the Kindle

Q. What font sizes are available on the Kindle and how do I change them?

A. See Choosing Among Six Font Sizes in Chapter III - Kindle Basics.

Q. How do I justify text on the Kindle screen, or get rid of text justification?

A. Press the aA key to bring up the "Adjust Font Size" screen, and press J as a show/hide toggle for text justification options.

Q. How do I bookmark a "page" while I am reading on the Kindle?

A. Press ALT-B. Pressing ALT-B again will get rid of the bookmark. A little graphic "dog-ear" at the upper right of the display screen signifies that a page is bookmarked. This bookmarking feature should not be confused with another bookmarking feature, in which the Kindle will always save the last "page" that you visited in any document, regardless of whether you leave the page by turning off the Kindle, running out of battery power, or to go to another document, to the Home screen, to the Kindle store, or anywhere else.

Q. I like to use my Kindle to read while I am on a cardio machine at the gym. Is there any way that I can move through a document without using my hands?

A. Yes. See "Slideshow" in Chapter X - More Kindle Tips and Tricks. Although you can't calibrate the "page-turning" speed with this feature, you may be able to approach the same issue, if your visual acuity permits, by ratcheting up or down the font size on the Kindle display.

Books and Other Content for the Kindle

Q. How many titles are available in the Kindle Store?

A. As of late August 2008, approximately 9 months after the Kindle's launch, there were 160,000 titles available under Kindle Books, 372 Kindle Blogs, 24 Kindle Newspapers, and 16 Kindle Magazines. Although the Kindle catalog grew rather slowly in the initial months after launch, it began growing at a far brisker pace -- about 25,000 new titles a month! -- by Summer 2008.

Q. How quickly can I expect to receive a Kindle edition on my Kindle after I make a purchase from the Kindle store?

A. Amazon's marketing claims are that you will generally receive your Kindle books via the Whispernet in about a minute, but the actual performance is usually much better. In a recent interview Jeff Bezos said that the mean Whispernet delivery time is 12 seconds. In my experience this standard also applies to delivery of Kindle content to your computer should you opt to receive it there and transfer it via USB to your Kindle.

Q. How do I download Kindle edition content to my Kindle when I am out of range of the wireless Whispernet service?

A. See Downloading Kindle Editions Via USB Cable in Chapter VII - Traveling with Your Kindle.

Q. It's all well and good to have 160,000 titles available for the Kindle, but that doesn't help me when there is a book I want to read on my Kindle and it is not available electronically. How can I let the publisher know?

A. For Kindle owners who search for titles that are not yet available in Kindle editions, Amazon now provides a handy little above-the-fold widget, complete with a miniature picture of a Kindle, allowing a single click to "Please tell the publisher: I'd like to read this book on Kindle." Just find the most recently published edition of the book and use this tool to give the publisher a heads up.

Q. Why do I have to pay for blogs on the Kindle when they are free on the web?

A. The blog subscriptions that are available in the Kindle Store are pushed directly to your Kindle without any advertising or any other revenue-producing architecture other than the relatively nominal monthly subscription charges, which provide an economic incentive for their authors and publishers to make this content available directly on the Kindle. That being said, it is also possible to read a lot of blog content at no charge on the Kindle by using RSS feeds or services such as Google Reader, as outlined in Chapter VI - Using Google Reader to Read Your Favorite Blogs on the Amazon Kindle.

Q. How can I find free content to read on my Kindle?

A. There are hundreds of thousands of free or "public domain" books, articles, and stories available for the Kindle. Two of the best websites for free content are Manybooks and Feedbooks. To learn more about these sites and get a link to a list of other free-content websites, see Great Sources for Free Books for Your Kindle in Chapter X - More Kindle Tips and Tricks.

Typing, Writing, Editing and Note-taking On the Kindle

Q. I'm so frustrated trying to learn to type with my thumbs! And when I do make a mistake and discover it 10 characters later there must be some way that I can get to the mistake and fix it without erasing everything I typed in the line since!

A. Just so. You can move the cursor left and right, one space at a time, without erasing any characters, by typing ALT-H to move the cursor to the left and ALT-J to move to the right. And of course, you can erase characters one at a time by using the backspace (<-) key at the right of the keyboard or erase the entire input field by holding down the ALT key and pressing that same backspace key.

Q. Is it true that there are a lot of characters available that don't show up on the keyboard?

A. Yes, just tap the SYM key from the bottom line of the keyboard while typing and the screen will display all the other symbols and characters that you may select by rolling the scrollwheel up or down and clicking on your selection.

For more information on how you can annotate, highlight, clip, save, edit, cut and paste from any Kindle document for research and other purposes, see Chapter VIII - **The Kindle as a Writing, Editing, and Publishing Device.**

Traveling with the Kindle

Q. Since there is no Kindle wireless service outside the United States, why would I want to carry the Kindle with me when traveling outside the country?

A. Ahhh, let me count the ways, or the reasons why, you should consider the Kindle indispensable for such trips. Once you travel with the Kindle, you will never want to travel without it. See Chapter VII - Traveling with Your Kindle.

Q. What's the real story on the GPS that is supposedly built into the Kindle?

A. Well, here's the scoop -- see The Kindle and GPS - Intriguing but Frustrating in Chapter VII - Traveling with Your Kindle. The only other thing I'll say is that you leave home expecting to rely solely on your Kindle for navigational purposes, you should also leave some instructions about when they should send out a search party.

Other Kindle Features

Q. How do I put the Kindle to sleep?

A. The Kindle will go into sleep mode after a brief period of inactivity, or by typing ALT-Aa

Q. How do I reboot or reset my Kindle?

A. In addition to simply turning the Kindle off and on again, there are several ways to reboot. From the keyboard, you can try holding down the ALT and SHIFT keys and typing R.

If the keyboard is frozen, you can do a hard reset using the reset pinhole under the Kindle's back cover. Keep a pushpin or paper clip handy for this purpose; trying to use a pen is problematic both because pen points are often too large for the pinhole and also because a pen may leave inky residue inside the Kindle.

If for any reason you are unable to access the pinhole, you can also achieve a hard reset by disconnecting and reconnecting, or replacing, your Kindle's battery. It is not advisable to use this approach except in a pinch.

All of these approaches except the on-off switch will wipe clean the Kindle's cache so that, for instance, you will have to type in user ID and password again before accessing a private account such as your Gmail account.

Q. Can I check the time on my Kindle?

A. Yes, just type ALT-T to get the time (text from Kindle document reader; numerical elsewhere). The time on your Kindle will reflect the time zone associated with the address linked to you Amazon account.

Q. Is it true that I can play video games on my Kindle?

A. Not quite. But if you really, really want to use your Kindle to play a game, you can start a game of "Minesweeper" by pressing ALT-SHIFT-M.

Q. How do I save and/or print a screenshot from my Kindle?

A. See Save and Print a Screenshot with Your Kindle in Chapter X - More Kindle Tips and Tricks.

Q. I love the Kindle's "search" feature but it would be nice to limit my searches and the amount of time they take. Can I do that?

A. Yes, you can limit your Kindle search to specific universes such as the Kindle Store, Wikipedia, or the web by typing your search term into the search field with the following prefixes separated by a space:

@web: Web Browser
@wiki: Wikipedia
@store: Kindle Store
@time: Time
@help: List of supported "@" shortcuts

Q. How do I set my own personal Kindle screen saver?

A. See Set a Personal Screen Saver in Chapter X - More Kindle Tips and Tricks.

Q. What's the best way for me to organize the content on my Kindle?

A. Content management architecture is by far the weakest link in Kindle 1.0. After you experience the pleasure of being able to order and download Kindle books and other content seamlessly within seconds, you will unfortunately have to put up with the opposite kind of experience when it comes to being able to manage and organize that same content on your own Kindle. Although the Kindle menu will direct you to something called Content Manager, it provides a slow and clunky process that you would be wise to avoid. Instead, Kindle owners who have installed SD cards will find it much easier and faster to connect their Kindles to their computers via USB cable and move content around on their Kindles and their SD cards with their computers' native storage drive and folder or directory management interfaces. While this much faster work-around will not allow you to create Kindle subfolders from which your Kindle can recognize and read content, you will, as one useful example, be able to organize off-Kindle content by subfolder on your SD card so that you can find it and return it to the Kindle-recognized "document" folder when you need it in the future. One can hope that Amazon will address the content management disaster in the next software version so that the fix can be applied to all Kindles.

Q. How do I use the Kindle for email?

A. See Chapter V - How to Use the Amazon Kindle for Email.

Q. I can see email messages on my Kindle but when I try to access them I get an error message. Can you help me figure out what I am doing wrong?

A. See Troubleshooting Tips if You Have Difficulty Accessing Gmail or Other Web Pages in Chapter V - How to Use the Amazon Kindle for Email.

Q. What are the wireless charges for data or any other charges that I am incurring for using the Kindle's web browser, how will I be billed, and how do I make payment?

A. There are no charges for these services. Or, to be more precise, any such charges are paid directly by Amazon. The only charges you will incur as a Kindle owner are your original purchase price (now $359) for the Kindle, and the specific price you pay for Kindle books, newspapers, magazines, and blogs. For more information about this free service, see Chapter IV - The Amazon Kindle Basic Web Wireless Service: Why It Is a Revolutionary Feature, and Why Amazon Should Keep It Free or Cheap.

For dozens of other tips and treats for Kindle users, see Chapter X - Chapter X - **More Kindle Tips and Tricks**.

The Future of the Kindle and E-Reading

Q. Why did Amazon launch the Kindle, and which is more important, the chicken or the egg?

A. See Why Did Amazon Launch the Kindle, and Which is More Important, the Chicken or the Egg? In Chapter II -- What is a Kindle?.

Q. How many Kindles has Amazon shipped?

A. Ah, that's the question, isn't it? Amazon isn't saying, but it is important for the simple reason that the success of and significant ongoing growth of the Kindle's installed base would have a positive domino effect on the growth of the Kindle catalog and on Amazon's ongoing commitment to, and support of the device. For my take on this important question, see the section entitled How Many Kindles? Estimating the Current and Future "Installed Base," and Why It Is Important in Chapter IX - Projecting a Kindle Future. I believe that the installed base reached the 300,000 mark in early Summer 2008, will pass one million early in 2009, and continue to grow from there. Other estimates I have seen have ranged from half a million Kindles now extant to as few as 10,000 or so, which would require that each Kindle owner would have already purchased 2 or 3 copies of this book, something (buying the same book multiple times for the same Kindle) that Amazon fortunately does not allow.

Q. How can I let Amazon know about features that I would like to see included in next-generation Kindles or bugs and problems that need to be addressed.

A. See Your Wish is Amazon's Command in Chapter X -- The Golden Age of Kindle 2.0 and Beyond.

Q. How can I be sure that my Kindle has been updated with the latest software version and any Kindle enhancements that it may be included in it.

A. See Updating the Latest Version of Your Kindle's Operating Software in Chapter III - - Kindle Basics.

Bonus Excerpt

If you are among the many Kindle owners who is passionate about the future of reading, literature, and the indie writing and publishing movement, we invite you to enjoy the following chapter excerpted from another new book from Stephen Windwalker, now available in **a Kindle edition**.

A bonus excerpt from

Beyond the Literary-Industrial Complex:

How Authors and Publishers Are Using the Amazon Kindle and Other New Technologies to Unleash an Indie Movement of Readers and Writers

By Stephen Windwalker

Chapter III.2

THE FEEDBACK IS THE FILTER: WHO WILL DISTINGUISH QUALITY IN AN INDIE PUBLISHING FUTURE?

Now that we have seen how technological advances such as the Kindle, CreateSpace, and [***insert Next Big Thing here***] make it possible for authors and independent publishers to bring their work to readers (and, yes, "to market") without any significant financial investment (except for the obvious fact that time is money), it is important to bring the focus back to where we started in this book: to issues of quality and distinction.

Have you ever wondered how, before the rise of the publishing industry and the ***New York Times Book Review***, cultures managed to confer distinction on quality literary work? Who told the Beowulf poet, if not to keep "writing," exactly, then at least to keep composing? Who told an earlier bard: "Keep up the fine work, Homer! You'll need a good editor, but I think I hear a single!"

The processes by which cultures filter and distinguish between quality artistic work and lesser efforts are constantly subject to their own reversals, second-guessing, and border wars. At times these processes are not so different either from a game of "king of the mountain" among ten-year-olds, or from the process by which religious sects confer the status of "messiah" or "madman" on someone who walks the earth making unexpected pronouncements.

One's acceptance (or not) of a jury's judgments will always be intrinsically tethered to, and will sometimes inform, one's considerations about that jury's composition. Controversies over who gets to serve as a culture's jury become especially fierce when the culture is undergoing major structural changes as a result of changes in audience, artistic process, and the means of production and dissemination employed by the culture's various media.

But this relationship between the "what's worth reading?" question and the question of "who thinks so?" is not a simple one. Even if we could agree on what constitutes excellent writing (which we can't), there would be myriad other considerations of lesser or greater importance to individual readers. Beyond the domain of the relatively small number of books that become bestsellers, there are hundreds of thousands of books and authors with smaller but still significant followings based on genre, topic, style, personal loyalties, their linkages with other books and reading communities, and, of course, their quality as received and registered by individual readers. In a "long-tail" literary world where there is a seemingly limitless choice of individual titles, what we must do to find the books that we want to read is changed dramatically and depends on the ways in which we, and the cultural marketplaces that we frequent, are organized into tribes and sub-tribes of readers and writers. But before we explore that Googlezon present and future, a look at where we have been may help us to be clear about what there is to lose and to gain in the transformations that are shaking the 21st-century publishing world.

In the grand early- and mid-20th century world of American publishing, the Olympian judgments of venerable publishing houses such as Scribners and Alfred Knopf were accepted, by and large, by writers, readers, and other gatekeepers and tastemakers of the book trade such as critics and booksellers. Most authors trusted editors and agents to give fair consideration to their submissions and to make selections that corresponded in some discernible way to their relative quality, even if anti-artistic censorship led occasionally to the temporary suppression of distinguished efforts such as ***Ulysses, Lolita, Lady Chatterley's Lover,*** or ***Howl***. The fact that the publishing industry was overwhelmingly a white man's world was but a sad mirror of similar barriers that flawed the society at large. And although it frequently did not deliver on its promises, "the life of the writer" often seemed to promise a way out of many ghettoes of race, gender, class, and psychopathology.

Authors such as Hemingway and Faulkner enjoyed special status as literary celebrities, with face time on the cover of ***Time*** and work excerpted or serialized in widely read magazines such as The ***Saturday Evening Post*** or ***Collier's***. This mass culture validated, reflected, and extended the literary culture, and several such authors enjoyed the kind of popular status that later became the terrain of rock stars, respected at times for literary achievement but just as often for their legends as rugged (or not) individualists who rose by their own remarkable efforts to live lives that inspired a kind of ***Lifestyles of the Literary Rich and Famous*** envy or emulation.

The fact that the mass culture was able to provide fair representation of the literary culture is testimony to the poverty of each in their common homogeneity. Still and all, 20th century literature often broadened and illuminated the human experience, helped us to fathom if not always to embrace the ghastly and lovely and banal range of human behavior, and seemed often to anticipate or give form to nearly every preoccupation of the species. The incubation and development of writers has never been precisely a democratic process, even with respect to opportunity, but these paths appeared accessible to so many that "to become a writer" became at once a lifestyle dream, a therapeutic cure (or enabler), and one of the world's most glorious and widely held career objectives. The overall selection processes seemed fair or seamless or logically Darwinian enough that both authors and audience tended to trust and accept the roles of editors, agents, and other gatekeepers. Such trust was based on several key assumptions:

· manuscripts submitted to agents and editors would usually get a reading, and a fair reading to boot;

· agents would make a serious effort to sell any work they arranged to represent;

· there would be a rough and uneven yet still plausible correspondence between those works accepted for publication and those deemed to have either literary quality or commercial viability or both, underpinned by a widely shared if sentimental trust that the publishing world was well-populated with individuals genuinely committed to pushing the equation whenever possible in the direction of literary quality; and

· once a book was accepted for publication, its publisher would make a serious effort to market it so that it would stand a fair chance of getting inclusion and notice in the thousands of independent bookstores that were as ubiquitous then as hardware stores and in the literary periodicals that reviewed a much larger selection of literary work than they consider nowadays.

None of the foregoing assumptions has survived recent dramatic changes in the publishing industry. Only a tiny percentage of outsiders' manuscript submissions sent to agents and editors gets even a cursory reading now. Pragmatic agents often see it as a quixotic enterprise even to submit literary fiction, narrative nonfiction, or other good work to the major publishing houses unless something about them nearly guarantees bestseller status. These houses are so driven by the need for scalable revenues and high turnover bestsellers that literary quality or enduring cultural value usually takes a distant back seat to considerations about whether an author has a marketable brand-name (think Paris Hilton, Danielle Steel, Jenna Jameson, or Tom Clancy) or a powerful cross-media sales platform (think Bill O'Reilly, Ann Coulter, Dr. Phil, or Sean Hannity).

These failures of the mainstream publishing industry and its gatekeepers to meet the cultural and economic needs of readers and writers might lead in any event to challenges to the traditional roles of judge and jury in our literary culture. But part of the publishing companies' power also accrues from a mighty self-censoring tendency among many writers, a walking-on-eggshells phenomenon that Jonathan Franzen, in his essay collection ***How to Be Alone***, has aptly described as "the idea … that cultural complaint is pathetic and self-serving in writers who don't sell, ungracious in writers who do."

Underlying these issues of fairness and sensibility is a more fundamental sea change that guarantees the continuing transformation of the publishing industry. Whatever its grandeur, much of American culture in the middle decades of the 20th century was built on assumptions of stunning homogeneity. In music, literature, film, television, and politics the only significant differences recognized by the mass culture were generational, and any cultural expressions on the "other" side of the culture's primary racial divides were, to white audiences, for all intents and purposes "underground."

In contrast, we now swim in a sea of limitless cultural choices. Although the explosions of the internet and digital technologies are the primary enabling forces for the existence of this long-tail world, its mere existence is not its most significant distinction. More importantly, a remarkable confluence of forces has created an active appetite for such a wide array of choices. These forces include the early indie movements in music and film, the political ferment of the sixties, changes in educational approach and, most importantly, the growth of the internet as a social and cultural networking infrastructure.

While the mainstream mega-publishers seem bound by economics and their own retrograde pre-occupation with bestsellers to fall short of satisfying the growing appetite for choice, independent publishers and entrepreneurial indie authors are well-situated to respond. Small, fast-moving publishers and authors can respond to niche needs and tribal tastes not only in fiction, poetry, and literary nonfiction but also in a wide array of other nonfiction categories.

At the most recent turn of the century, important advances in technology and the marketplace were empowering independent-minded writers and pushing the publishing world toward, if not a precipice, a significant tipping point:

· First, digitized print technologies made quality short-run book manufacturing so inexpensive that an independent publisher could surpass the production break-even point with a printing of 2,000 to 3,000 copies of a paperback original and a sell-through of as few as a third of the print run; and

· second, such publishers gained easy, inexpensive access to a gathering critical mass of sales and distribution channels including their own websites, the Amazon Advantage program, the Internet's thousands of independent third-party booksellers, and a critical mass of independent bookstores and libraries. Wholesalers such as Baker & Taylor and Quality Books began to work proactively with small publishers and some short-run book manufacturers began to offer their small-publisher customers reliable bundles of ancillary services such as warehousing, fulfillment, distribution, order processing, regular inventory and sales reporting, and collections.

More recent developments have only intensified the velocity of change: with the advent of the Amazon Kindle and Amazon's CreateSpace publishing platform in 2007, authors and publishers can bring literature "to market" at little or no cost, and even more importantly, with immediate connectivity to potent established markets and distribution channels that lead to millions of readers.

Each of these developments is likely to subvert traditional gatekeeping roles in the publishing industry. Will they also subvert the literary culture itself by committing it to a relentless downward spiral in quality, cheapening and "democratizing" what is available in book or any other form to the point where quality written work goes begging because it is lost in a swamp of mediocrity? Although I personally welcome, and include myself in the ranks of, an independent publishing movement, I do not diminish the importance or reasonableness of this concern about quality. I must admit to being less sanguine on this issue than former Random House editor Jason Epstein, one of the most respected elders of the American publishing industry, who wrote in his thoughtful 2001 volume, ***Book Business: Publishing Past Present Future***, that "these new technologies will test the human capacity to distinguish value from a wilderness of choice, but humanity has always faced this dilemma and solved it well enough over time.... The filter that distinguishes value is a function of human nature, not of particular technologies."

But we are fortunate to have particular technologies to give human nature an assist. The internet offers a viral post-advertising expansion of communication channels and platforms by which readers may communicate not only with each other but also interactively with writers, publishers, booksellers, and librarians about the content and quality of books and other media. Within these protean networks all advertising is forbidden but almost any medium can carry, in its DNA, an acceptable alternative to marketing.

There is much for an indie publishing movement to emulate in the processes by which the "do-it-yourself" spirit in music and film during the last two or three decades has broken through to build a kind of positive if generic "brand" distinction for "indie" maverick movements in their own right, as compared with the self-publisher's "vanity press" stigma that must be overcome by independent book publishers. It is no accident that one of the more articulate voices promoting an indie book publishing movement, editor-in-chief Johnny Temple of Akashic Books, would write in a recent ***Poets & Writers*** article that "I entered the book business through the portal of underground rock music.

"The idea," wrote Temple in describing the musicians' indie movement, "was that hardworking bands, upstart record labels (often launched by musicians) and dedicated fans could forge a vital, idealistic alternative to the mainstream music business." The importance of those "dedicated fans" should not be underestimated; writers, publishers, booksellers, librarians, and mindful readers should seek out every available opportunity to cultivate vehicles for reader communication, reader-writer contact, and reader self-identification with an indie movement of writers and publishers. Both in the physical world of reading groups, bookstore readings, library discussion groups, and Oprah segments and in the web world of book blogs, meet-ups, online social networking sites and Amazon customer reviews, the potential for such interaction is exploding far more dramatically than the population base of physical or digital book readers is atrophying. Writers' groups, which tend as it is to function simultaneously as readers' groups, would do well to seek out any chance to broaden their base and replicate or extend themselves as reader-writer affinity groups. One can easily imagine the Kindle itself, with its huge (and mostly still untapped) potential for file-sharing, annotation, and networking, as a primary hub for such communities if future price breaks and next-generation input enhancements allow.

Even in a cultural environment such as the blogosphere -- a seeming narcissist's paradise where the ego-gratification of traffic and comment is instant and almost every reader is also a writer -- literary culture is braced by forces that are, in one sense, as old-fashioned as book discussion groups or the knowledgeable independent bookseller whose recommendations join her wide reading experience with her understanding of her customers' reading interests and tastes. Yet as old-school as they may be in basic form, the internet recapitulators of these natural outcroppings of human nature can be almost unimaginably more powerful because they are also viral, instantaneous, and global.

Readers and book browsers in every age have wanted to know, in evaluating whether to take a chance (either with their time or their money, or both) on a book, how many others are reading it, who they are, and what they think of it. This information serves not only to send signals about quality; it also feeds a deep and powerful tribal urge for many readers. They want to read books (or see movies or hear music) that will spark and perhaps elevate their social and intellectual interactions with others, and when they read good books they want to seek out people with whom they can discuss the books, their ideas, their characters, and so forth. Disclosing one's reading, musical, and film tastes has become such an automatic self-branding ritual that, in addition to helping to bring you new recommendations for a book to read on Sunday morning, the act may also help you to find a date on Saturday night.

Just as buzz breeds buzz, the process by which sales success breeds sales success is not limited to those permutations that involve readers (or all the book trade's gatekeepers) noting a title on the ***New York Times*** bestseller list and then making room for it in their own plans. On the internet, whether in book blogs, among the apparently democratic and accessible book review and rating templates to be found on Amazon.com or its emulators, or in countless other venues yet to be imagined, the information that a title is selling well is instantly available, easy to use, and all the more likely, because of its own seemingly transparent and unmediated character, to serve as a quality filter or signaling system for readers and for all the other aforementioned gatekeepers of the book trade. The natural consequence of these processes in our hit-obsessed culture will be to ensure that we will always have bestsellers, perhaps even long after we have book publishers in the traditional sense, even if over time the sales requirements for attaining such status are somewhat moderated.

For all of its fertility as a vineyard for individual creativity and differentiated voices, the web is also an elegantly complex yet exquisitely simple binary world where, as with the inner meta-biology of the human brain, content and process may eventually be equivalent. Every word that is typed, read, linked, or clicked becomes traffic and velocity, and every hit is its own unmediated form of comment, and therefore of content. Every time we tag, visit, rate, buy, link, bookmark, download, sample or otherwise engage content, let alone when we write a comment or customer review or include it in our blog or blogroll, we are buzzing: asserting that certain content appeals to us or appalls us or bores us and may have a similar effect on others in the various tribes or networks to which we belong. We often choose these groups on the basis of the shared appeal of certain content; indeed they often spring up on an ad hoc basis around certain authors or books, certain musicians or films, etc. Importantly, given the leisure-time deficits with which many of us live, the bar of participation can be set as high or as low as we like.

These processes are as important for audience as they are for artists. It is obviously my intention here to be an advocate for the kind of cultural citizenship or activism that helps to define and organize the tribes and literary affinity groups of which we have been speaking, and to sort and distinguish the work of authors and other creators. I will always encourage people to exercise their rights as audience members in these ways and to recognize that the infrastructures of Amazon, Google, YouTube, iTunes, MySpace and countless other websites are so effective and seamless that -- in ways that are so automatic that they may deserve the phrase "whether we like it or not" -- we are all buzz agents.

What was that I called you? Well, pardon my presumption. You may not have a marketing bone in your body, but you are a rare individual if you haven't weighed in with others on a few of the following topics: books, politics, music, film, cars, television, technology, destinations, sneakers, swimming holes, food, restaurants, bars, businesses, business models, magazines, babysitters, schools, fashion, driving directions, or plumbers. We learn early on how to influence others and how to find value for ourselves in the influence of others, with varying degrees of mindfulness and vigilance about the process depending on the forum in which it is occurring, the self-presentation of others, and our individual natures. Increasingly, as our culture gets meaner and more cynical, we are distrustful of influences that appear to be directly commercial, only to find that the marketing wizards are spending billions on buzz that is indirectly commercial. We may think that it is at the point when we have to stop and apply a bullshit detector to all this buzz that we have left Eden, but the truth is that we have not been to Eden for a while.

Being a lover of books and reading, a bibliophile, early in the 21st Century, often means being a pro-active and curious inquisitor, scouting out writers that appeal to you among the offerings of trusted authors, small presses and literary magazines, the remaining independent bookstores, reading groups, Amazon reviews, and book blogs. It often means making early commitments to the careers of authors you love and tracking every printed or digitized word they produce. It may even mean giving up a smidgen of your intellectual privacy, whether to your local bookseller or librarian or to the algorithm aces at Amazon.com, in order to allow them to use their gifts at what the marketing mavens call "collaborative filtering" to help you, who loved the book of Richard Ford stories you read on the beach last summer, to find a Ray Carver selection to read this summer.

I have no doubt, as one who has satisfied his own reading appetites through various combinations of these and other means for the past few decades, that a large part of what motivates us as book scouts and buzz agents is the joy of discovery and then the gratification and validation of sharing what we discover with those with whom we sense some common ground: "Eureka! I've been reading the most wonderful book! I'll pass it on to you as soon as I've finished." However much we may experience the reading itself as either solitary or, in connection with the author, dyadic, it can also become, with our bibliophile soul mates, satisfyingly social. And in our internet age, we can carry out these interactions either locally or globally.

As with most other scouting enterprises, scouting for good books to read -- and especially for books that suit our very individual reading needs -- is often a two-way street. The more we "speak," the more we will "hear." The more we listen, the more we will know about who we want to speak to, what to say to them, and what to ask them about. Along the way, we even learn a fair amount about how to conduct the conversation. One of the remarkable things about cultural marketplaces such as Amazon is the way in which they seem to train their visitors to become better and better at using the wealth of material that exists there to get their needs met.

Of course, to raise concerns about quality as if they only applied to the new forces in publishing is to beg the question regarding the performance of the traditional publishing institutions as defenders of literary quality. I am far from being the first writer to experience the relationships between authors (or, for that matter, readers) and the mainstream publishing industry as adversarial. I suspect that most of us, either chronically or episodically, are inclined to view almost anyone who tries to regulate our creative and cultural lives with some mixture of annoyance and contempt. If the issues that annoy us seem increasingly to be systemic rather than personal, then it is entirely appropriate for us to develop a sense of mission about the need to make things right. The mainstream publishing industry and its more Olympian apologists may prefer to cast such struggles as occurring between the guardians of publishing excellence and the rabble of artistic democracy, with the subtext that those in control, as much as they might like to suffer a thousand new flowers to bloom each publishing season, are, at the end of the day, the last remaining protectors of literary quality.

But all one must do is look around, in any chain bookstore or on the latest bestseller list, to conclude that, while the mainstream publishing industry may in some places have the elitist trappings of snobbish self-importance, it is not meritocratic in any way that is connected to literary quality. We note, without taking any pleasure in it, the fact that the quality filtering process that helped to make a bestseller of such a magnus opus as Jenna Jameson's ***How to Make Love Like a Porn Star*** or the latest scribblings of Paris Hilton or Rush Limbaugh is something less than meritocratic to begin with.

Once one determines that the big publishers could care less about quality at the expense of blockbuster bestsellers, it follows naturally that any renegade movement to allow independent creative people to make more of the decisions about what to publish and how to get that product into the hands of interested and discerning readers could be, and should be, less about artistic democracy than about artistic meritocracy and literary freedom. As growing numbers of writers accept the gifts and challenges of new technologies and our ubiquitous American entrepreneurial spirit and embark upon non-traditional publishing ventures to get their work before the reading public, we would be wise not to leave these issues of quality filtering, of "the cream rising to the top," either to the happenstances of human nature or to the vagaries of an untended marketplace. Along the way, some of us will be able to bring the universe of choices into smaller scale by connecting, if you will excuse my overburdening of that "cream to the top" metaphor, with consumers who prefer soy milk, goat's milk, buttermilk, and so forth.

For the self-interested author who believes that she has just self-published the next Great American Novel, the admonition in the previous paragraph may seem to be just another way of saying, "Don't just sit back and wait for the orders to start rolling in." But I mean to make a broader point: readers and writers, and especially those of us who locate ourselves vocationally anywhere in the literary culture, stand to benefit both directly and in a more general cultural sense by doing all we can to nurture those networks and informal associations that in one way or another honor, advance, and extend the market viability of literary work of distinction, of writing that is thoughtful, interesting, edgy, experimental, or, in the best sense of the word, ambitious. Perhaps this has always been true, but the stakes are higher now because the publishing industry at large is failing so miserably at these tasks and because, to be blunt, of the sheer volume of choices when something in the ballpark of 300,000 new titles is being printed each year.

There is already quite enough angst and hand-wringing about this flooding of the marketplace; I don't mean to suggest that any of us should posture or anoint ourselves as some sort of high-culture quality police. We can celebrate the candles without cursing the darkness, and I am much more troubled personally by the market flooding that is the result of the vast overprintings of individual titles, to the detriment both of the planet and of that quaint old phenomenon known as the mid-list title.

From here onward, there will be many good works, some in book form and some in shorter form that, because of the opportunities provided through the Kindle, the CreateSpace print-on-demand feature, and other yet-to-be-realized technologies, will be available "forever" and, absent any marketing, will sell usually in trickles of one or two each month, several each quarter. We can embrace this good fortune and, at the same time, be pleased that, much further out along the farthest reaches of the long tail, there will be works of the least significance and distinction, supported by the weakest of networks or no networks at all, that will exist only as onesies, twosies, or seldom-transmitted digital files. In the utter absence of buzz, quality, or usefulness, there will be only the sound of trees not having to fall in the forest because there is nobody there.

The moment may even come, as the role of the large commercially drive publishers declines, when one of those unreadable and unsellable titles will indeed be one that in another era might have been printed, remaindered, and ultimately destroyed by the hundreds of thousands. Of course we will never know when that elegantly silent moment occurs, but even without our being able to circle a date, I suggest that we should be able to celebrate its advent.

Made in the USA